THE CASEY ANTHONY MURDER CASE

BY ASHLEY STORM

AMERICAN CRIME STORIES

Essential Library

An Imprint of Abdo Publishing | abdobooks.com

ABDOBOOKS.COM

Published by Abdo Publishing, a division of ABDO, PO Box 398166, Minneapolis, Minnesota 55439. Copyright © 2024 by Abdo Consulting Group, Inc. International copyrights reserved in all countries. No part of this book may be reproduced in any form without written permission from the publisher. Essential Library™ is a trademark and logo of Abdo Publishing.

Printed in the United States of America, North Mankato, Minnesota.
102023
012024

THIS BOOK CONTAINS RECYCLED MATERIALS

Cover Photo: Red Huber/Pool/Getty Images News/Getty Images
Interior Photos: ZUMA Press, Inc./Alamy, 5, 47; Red Line Editorial, 7; Red Huber/Orlando Sentinel/Tribune News Service/Getty Images, 11, 21, 62; Orlando Sentinel/Tribune News Service/Getty Images, 12; Red Huber/Pool/Orlando Sentinel/AP Images, 15, 16, 54, 59, 75, 78, 81; Joe Burbank/Pool/Orlando Sentinel/AP Images, 19, 50, 64–65, 73; Joe Raedle/Getty Images News/Getty Images, 22–23, 96; Ricardo Ramirez Buxeda/Orlando Sentinel/Tribune News Service/Getty Images, 27; Joe Chansak/Shutterstock Images, 30; John Raoux/AP Images, 33, 45; Archive PL/Alamy, 34; Phelan M. Ebenhack/AP Images, 37, 40, 41, 91; Joe Burbank/Pool/Getty Images News/Getty Images, 53; Phelan Ebenhack/ZUMA Press, Inc./Alamy, 57; Shutterstock Images, 69; Joe Burbank/Orlando Sentinel/Tribune News Service/Getty Images, 71; Alan Diaz/AP Images, 85; Joshua Replogle/AP Images, 94

Editor: Laura Stickney
Series Designer: Melissa Martin

Library of Congress Control Number: 2023939439

PUBLISHER'S CATALOGING-IN-PUBLICATION DATA

Names: Storm, Ashley, author.
Title: The Casey Anthony murder case / by Ashley Storm
Description: Minneapolis, Minnesota: Abdo Publishing, 2024 | Series: American crime stories | Includes online resources and index.
Identifiers: ISBN 9781098292096 (lib. bdg.) | ISBN 9798384910039 (ebook)
Subjects: LCSH: Crime and criminals--Juvenile literature. | Killing (Murder)--Juvenile literature. | United States--Juvenile literature. | Anthony, Casey, 1986- --Juvenile literature. | Florida--Juvenile literature. | Anthony, Caylee, 2005-2008--Juvenile literature. | Children--Crimes against--Juvenile literature.
Classification: DDC 364.97--dc23

CONTENTS

This book discusses accounts of crime, violence, and death that may be disturbing to some readers.

CHAPTER ONE
A MISSING CHILD
4

CHAPTER TWO
SUMMER OF FUN
14

CHAPTER THREE
WEB OF LIES
26

CHAPTER FOUR
MEDIA FRENZY
36

CHAPTER FIVE
THE TRIAL BEGINS
46

CHAPTER SIX
WHITE PONTIAC SUNFIRE
56

CHAPTER SEVEN
HOMICIDE BY UNDETERMINED MEANS
70

CHAPTER EIGHT
THE VERDICTS
80

CHAPTER NINE
THE AFTERMATH
90

Timeline	98	Source Notes	106
Essential Facts	100	Index	110
Glossary	102	About the Author	112
Additional Resources	104		

CHAPTER ONE

A MISSING CHILD

On August 11, 2008, Orange County water meter reader Roy Kronk and two coworkers stepped into a wooded area alongside Suburban Drive in Orlando, Florida. The shade of the trees offered a welcome respite from the sweltering summer heat. Kronk scanned the area for a private place to relieve himself. As he moved away from his coworkers, his eyes settled on something strange in the distance. A tree had fallen in a wet, swampy area of the woods. Near the tree, there was a gray bag on the ground. Trash in the swamp wasn't uncommon, but an unusual object caught Kronk's attention. Round and white, it appeared to be a human skull.

Kronk told his coworkers that he'd seen something odd and attempted to point it out to them. But the other men were distracted by a large dead rattlesnake they'd found in

Caylee Anthony's remains were found in a heavily wooded wetland area just off the side of the road. The site was only about a five-minute walk away from the Anthony home.

> ## CARRION EATERS
>
> Many factors play a role in how quickly a body decomposes. One of the biggest factors is whether the body is exposed to organisms that eat dead things. Carrion eaters, such as vultures and crows, act as nature's cleanup crew. They eat dead animals, picking the flesh from their bones. Opportunistic feeders such as opossums and raccoons help too. But bugs play the biggest role in decomposition. A single fly will lay hundreds of eggs, using a dead body as a host and food source for its young.

the woods. When the workers headed back to their vehicle, they took the snake with them. For the rest of the day, Kronk and his coworkers played with, showed off, and took pictures with the snake.

Later that evening, Kronk thought about what he had seen in the swamp. On the news, he'd heard that a search was underway for a missing toddler from the area. Two-year-old Caylee Anthony had been missing since June. Her mother, Casey Anthony, had been charged with felony child neglect, lying to police, and obstructing an investigation. The investigating officers believed the child was dead.

It occurred to Kronk that the swampland was the perfect place to hide a body. Not only were people unlikely to venture into the swamp but the stench of decaying plants and swamp gas could mask the smell of a body decomposing. Kronk called the police to report what he'd seen. Two days later, two police deputies met Kronk on Suburban Drive. After glancing around

DISCOVERING CAYLEE'S REMAINS

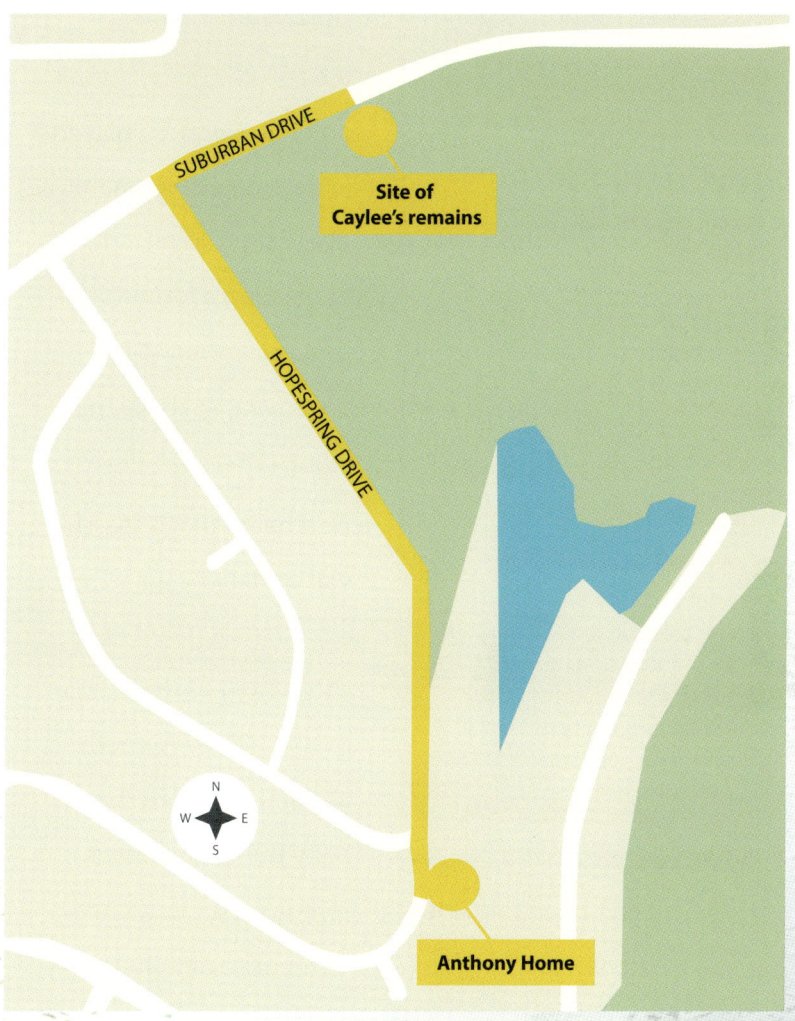

Caylee Anthony's remains were found less than half a mile (0.8 km) from George and Cindy Anthony's house. Her remains were only 19 feet (5.8 m) away from the road.[1]

the area and seeing nothing out of the ordinary, they berated Kronk for wasting their time. They did not venture into the swamp for a better look. It would be another four months before Caylee Anthony's bones were discovered there.

Teenage Mother

In 2005, 18-year-old Casey Anthony was keeping a big secret: she was pregnant. Nobody noticed Casey's protruding stomach until she attended her uncle's wedding wearing a formfitting dress. People realized not only that Casey was going to have a baby but also that the baby would be arriving soon. By this point, Casey was already in her third trimester of pregnancy.

A family member confronted Casey's mother, Cindy Anthony, about Casey's obvious baby bump and asked why they hadn't been told about the pregnancy. Cindy shook her head in denial. In Cindy's mind, her teenage daughter couldn't be pregnant because she wasn't in a relationship with anyone. Casey's father, George Anthony, had noticed his daughter's changing body. Deep down, he suspected she might be pregnant. But like Cindy, he rationalized the signs away,

> Casey did not have enough credits to graduate from high school, but she didn't tell her parents. They attended her high school graduation ceremony only to discover that Casey wasn't among the graduates.

telling himself that Casey had simply gained weight.

Two weeks after her uncle's wedding, Casey confessed to her parents that she was in fact pregnant. Despite their concerns about their teenage daughter being a single parent, Cindy and George were excited about the new addition to their family. Cindy purchased maternity clothes, organized a baby shower, and bought toys for the baby. George and Cindy turned their computer room into a nursery. Since Casey already owned several Winnie the Pooh items, the Anthonys chose the popular children's book character as the theme for the baby's room. Less than two months after George and Cindy learned they were going to be grandparents, Casey gave birth to their granddaughter, Caylee Marie Anthony.

> ## A POTENTIAL FATHER
>
> When Casey confirmed her pregnancy, she told Jesse Grund that he was the baby's father. He was skeptical since Casey's due date was less than nine months from when they'd met. But Jesse cared for Casey, so he decided to stand in as the father-to-be. After Caylee was born, a paternity test confirmed that Jesse was not Caylee's father. But Jesse didn't care. He proposed to Casey a few months after Caylee's birth, on New Year's Eve. But by the following May, Casey ended the engagement. According to Jesse, Casey's reason for the breakup was that Jesse loved Caylee more than he loved her.

The identity of Caylee Anthony's father is unknown.

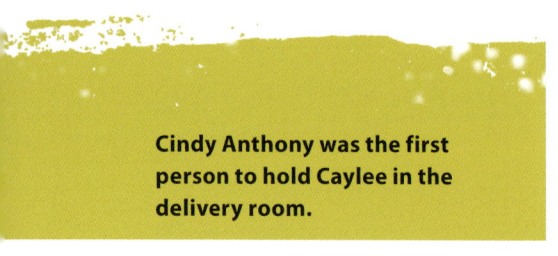

Cindy Anthony was the first person to hold Caylee in the delivery room.

Over time, the relationship between Cindy and Casey grew strained. Cindy would frequently back out of babysitting agreements after promising Casey that she'd watch Caylee. Cindy also criticized Casey's parenting skills, even calling her an unfit mother on one occasion. Casey confided in her friend Amy Huizenga, saying that her mother's comment had really upset her.

Later, Huizenga would describe Casey and Cindy's difficult relationship. "It was hard. Her mom was continually agitated with her," she said.[2] In the spring of 2008, tensions between Casey and Cindy reached a breaking point. Casey began to pull away from Cindy, spending less time with her. Casey and Caylee began staying at friends' apartments more often.

A Typical Morning

On June 16, 2008, George Anthony was watching *Diners, Drive-Ins and Dives* on television when his two-year-old granddaughter, Caylee, bounded into the room. She was wearing denim shorts, a pink shirt, pink socks, and white sandals and sunglasses. A bookbag was strapped to her back. Bubbling with excitement, Caylee told her grandfather she was going to see Zanny. Zanny was a familiar name in the Anthony household. Though George had never met Zanny, he

A photo used as evidence in Casey's trial shows Casey, *left*, when she was pregnant. Casey's brother, Lee, said that he wasn't told about the pregnancy until days before Caylee was born.

knew that she was Caylee's longtime babysitter. "Zanny" was Caylee's nickname for her.

A few minutes later, George watched as Casey opened the back passenger-side door to her white Pontiac Sunfire and

Members of Caylee Anthony's family said she had a big personality. She loved Winnie the Pooh and had a favorite doll, which her grandmother later found inside the white Pontiac Sunfire.

buckled Caylee into her car seat. He blew Caylee a kiss goodbye. It was a typical morning, just like so many others. But every detail of that day is etched into George's memory. It was the last time he saw his granddaughter alive.

CAYLEE MARIE ANTHONY

Caylee was a vibrant, playful toddler who loved to swim, dance, and sing along to her favorite song, "You Are My Sunshine." Her disappearance captivated the hearts and minds of people around the world. When Caylee's death was confirmed, more than a thousand mourners traveled to Florida for her memorial service at First Baptist Church in Orlando. In the words of Pastor David Uth, the mourners had gathered "to celebrate the gift of Caylee Anthony. Though short, her life made a huge impact on many people."[3]

CHAPTER TWO

SUMMER OF FUN

When George said goodbye to Caylee on June 16, 2008, it was the last time he—or anyone else—would report seeing the girl alive. That evening, Casey went to a Blockbuster video store with her boyfriend, college student and club promoter Anthony "Tony" Lazzaro. Surveillance footage from the store showed Casey and Lazzaro walking with their arms wrapped around each other affectionately. Caylee wasn't with them.

For the next month, Casey avoided her parents, opting to spend more time with her friends, boyfriend, and roommates. She lived her life as though nothing were out of the ordinary. She moved in to her boyfriend's apartment, went on shopping trips to Target and JCPenney, cooked meals for Lazzaro and his roommates, and went to bars with her friends. Casey didn't tell a single person that Caylee was missing.

Photos from the time when Caylee was missing show Casey going on dates with her boyfriend, partying at bars, and shopping. These photos were later used as evidence against Casey.

"Bella Vita"

On June 20, Casey partied with friends at Fusion Nightclub in Orlando. She laughed as she danced. Casey also competed in a "hot body" contest, posing for photographs and dancing provocatively on stage with other women.[1] To her friends and others at the bar, including the "shot girls" who carried trays of drinks to customers, Casey looked like she was having the time of her life. For the rest of

Shortly before Caylee disappeared, Casey sent her boyfriend an instant message in which she called Caylee "little snot head" and said that spending the day with her was exhausting.[2]

Tattoo artist Bobby Williams reported that Casey seemed happy and never mentioned Caylee when she came into the shop to get her "Bella Vita" tattoo.

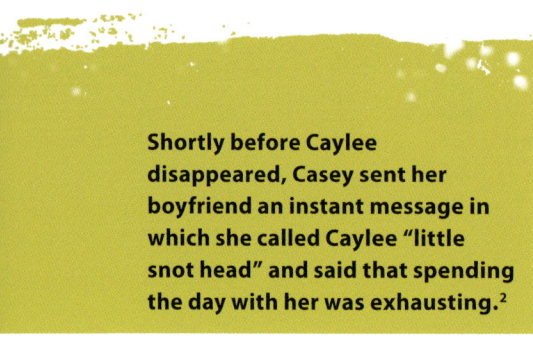

June and through the first half of July, Casey appeared to be happy. Lazzaro thought she was the perfect girlfriend, and his roommates enjoyed having Casey around because she cooked and cleaned.

On July 2, Casey went to Cast Iron Tattoos in Orlando and met with tattoo artist Bobby Williams. Williams had known Casey for seven years. Nothing about Casey seemed unusual on this occasion. She didn't seem sad or upset. After a quick consultation and a few minutes of drafting a tattoo design for Casey, Williams inked the piece onto Casey's back. In stylized, swirly lettering, the words *Bella Vita* were tattooed onto her left shoulder blade, surrounded by stars. These words are Italian for "beautiful life."

A LOVING MOTHER

Prosecutors in Casey's eventual trial did not present any witness testimony that she was a bad mother to Caylee. On the contrary, multiple witnesses testified that Casey was a loving and attentive mother to her toddler. Even Cindy, who had tended to criticize her daughter while Caylee was alive, testified that "Casey was a very loving, very caring mother. She had a very easy, very quick maternal instinct that was very evident as soon as Caylee was born."[3]

Excuse after Excuse

Between mid-June and mid-July, Casey's friends began to wonder why Caylee hadn't been around. One of Lazzaro's roommates, Cameron Campana, had previously babysat Caylee.

He liked the toddler. She was a fun, smart kid who could count to ten in Spanish—something Campana could not do himself. Every time Campana asked Casey why he hadn't seen Caylee at the apartment, Casey offered a reasonable excuse. She would say that Caylee was with her nanny, Zanny, at the beach or at one of Orlando's theme parks.

When Caylee wasn't with Zanny, Casey said the child was with her grandparents. Having no reason to suspect that anything was wrong, the roommates accepted Casey's excuses. After all, she was the same old Casey as always. Her personality hadn't changed at all.

Nathan Lezniewicz, another friend of Casey's at the time, described her as an extrovert who "liked to have a good time."[4] Lezniewicz would later testify at Casey's trial, saying that at the time, there was no sign that anything was going on. None of Casey's friends were concerned that they hadn't seen Caylee recently. They all believed the girl was in the care of a responsible adult.

> ### IMPOSSIBLE QUESTIONS
>
> Years after Caylee's disappearance, Casey's former friend Cameron Campana was still plagued with questions and doubts. In the weeks following Caylee's disappearance, Casey seemed like her usual self. But Campana wondered if he should have noticed that something was wrong, or if there were red flags that he missed. In a 2023 interview with the *U.S. Sun*, Campana said, "It used to drive me crazy thinking about the what-ifs. It still bothers me."[5]

Caylee was Cindy and George Anthony's only grandchild at the time. She called them "Cee Cee" and "Jo Jo."

But Casey's friends weren't the only ones who noticed Caylee's absence. Caylee's grandmother Cindy grew increasingly upset as time passed without any visits from Casey and Caylee. Cindy hadn't even been able to talk to Caylee on the telephone. Whenever she called to ask Casey to let her talk to Caylee, Casey always had an excuse for why Caylee wasn't available. Most of the time, she told Cindy the same thing she'd told her friends: Caylee was with Zanny.

Sometimes Casey claimed that she and Caylee were out of town. On the same day Casey was competing in the hot body contest at Fusion Nightclub, she lied to Cindy. She said she and Caylee were in Tampa, Florida, spending time with a colleague and her child. At one point, Casey said Zanny had been in an accident and needed Casey to stay with her for a while. On another occasion, she told Cindy that she and Caylee were in Jacksonville, Florida. Casey always had an excuse ready, but Cindy was running out of patience. She missed her granddaughter and was determined to see her. Casey's summer of fun was about to come to an end.

Three 911 Calls

When Cindy awoke on July 15, she had no idea that she would make three calls to 911 by the end of the day. She also didn't expect she would initiate a missing person report that would lead to one of the nation's most publicized trials. The day's troubles began with a notification from the local impound lot. A vehicle owned by Cindy and her husband, George, was found abandoned in a parking lot and had been towed and impounded. The car was a white Pontiac Sunfire.

The Anthonys had given 22-year-old Casey permission to use the car as her personal vehicle. Cindy and George were not pleased that she'd abandoned it. They were also unhappy that it cost them a large sum of money to get the vehicle released from the impound lot. Even worse, the car reeked. A bag of rotting garbage had been left in the trunk for several weeks. The stench was so bad that Cindy would later tell the 911 dispatcher, "It smells like there's been a dead body in the d— car."[6]

After being denied visits with her granddaughter for more than a month, the impounded car was the final straw for Cindy. She got in touch with Amy Huizenga, one of Casey's closest friends, to help her track down Casey's whereabouts. With Huizenga's help, Cindy found Casey at Lazzaro's apartment.

Casey abandoned her white Pontiac Sunfire on June 27. It sat in the impound lot for about two weeks before George and Cindy were notified about it.

George and Cindy Anthony's house was located on Hopespring Drive in an Orlando suburb.

Cindy was upset to discover that her granddaughter wasn't at the apartment with Casey. She angrily demanded that Casey take her to see Caylee.

Casey told her that Caylee was with her nanny and that it was too late in the evening to pick her up. Cindy would not take no for an answer, so Casey left Lazzaro's apartment with her.

But once they were in Cindy's car, Casey refused to give her mother directions to the nanny's house to pick up Caylee. Frustrated, Cindy placed her first 911 call from the car.

"I want to bring her in," Cindy told the 911 dispatcher. "I want to press charges." While talking to the dispatcher, Cindy claimed that Casey had committed "grand theft" of the Pontiac Sunfire.[7] The dispatcher informed Cindy that the sheriff's department would have jurisdiction. While the dispatcher connected the call to another department, Cindy and Casey were recorded arguing in the background. Casey asked Cindy to wait for one more day, and Cindy responded that she'd already waited a month.

After hanging up with the dispatcher, Cindy continued to drive around while attempting to persuade Casey to give her directions to wherever Caylee was staying with Zanny. After failing to get any information out of Casey, Cindy drove home, bringing her daughter with her. Once inside her house, Cindy placed a second call to 911.

She asked that an officer be sent to her home. "I have someone here that I need to be arrested," she said, still referencing the stolen vehicle, "and I have a possible missing child."[8] In a frustrated but calm voice, Cindy explained that she had not seen Caylee in more than a month. The dispatcher said that an officer would be sent to the home, and the call was disconnected.

Before an officer arrived, Cindy made a third call to 911. In this call, her tone changed from frustrated to desperate.

> On July 15, 2008, Casey told the police that Caylee had been missing for 31 days. But George reported last seeing Caylee with Casey on June 16, 29 days earlier.

A RELUCTANT GRIEVER?

Law enforcement, the media, and the public speculated that Casey did not behave like a grieving mother while her daughter was missing. She seemed unconcerned and calm. And instead of notifying anyone that Caylee was missing, she spent her time partying and having fun. Because of this, many people suspected Casey of being involved in her daughter's death. But others argued that everyone grieves differently. During Casey's trial, grief expert Dr. Sally Karioth noted that young adults can sometimes be "reluctant grievers."[11] In a situation like Casey's, a person may resort to denial and act as if nothing has happened. Karioth also pointed out that this kind of behavior is common in people from families who don't communicate well or share their feelings.

As Cindy sobbed into the phone, the dispatcher attempted to figure out the situation. It quickly became evident that something was very wrong.

"I found out my granddaughter has been taken," Cindy sobbed. "My daughter finally admitted that the babysitter stole her!"[9] Cindy grew more difficult to understand, so the dispatcher asked to speak directly to Casey. Reluctantly, Casey took the phone.

Casey's voice contrasted with her mother's. While Cindy was inconsolable, Casey's voice was calm. Her words were crystal clear when she told the dispatcher, "My daughter's been missing for the last 31 days."[10]

CHAPTER THREE

WEB OF LIES

When Casey talked to the 911 dispatcher on July 15, 2008, she said she hadn't seen her daughter in 31 days. But she claimed that she knew who had taken her: Zenaida Fernandez-Gonzalez. This was Caylee's babysitter, also known as "Zanny the nanny."

Casey told the investigating officers that she'd been introduced to Zenaida two years earlier by her friend Jeffrey Hopkins, a wealthy man who worked for Nickelodeon and had a young son named Zachary. Zenaida had been babysitting for Caylee ever since. When the officers asked for Hopkins's contact information, Casey told them that his telephone number had been changed.

Later, investigators discovered that everything Casey told them about Hopkins was a lie. She had gone to middle school with a person named Jeffrey Hopkins but had not seen him or spoken to him in years. Although Hopkins was a real person, he

Ron Stucker, Chief of Criminal Investigations at the Orange County Sheriff's Office, spoke about the Anthony case at press conferences. He said Casey gave detectives conflicting information.

had not worked for Nickelodeon, did not know anyone named Zenaida Fernandez-Gonzalez, and did not have any children. If Casey had lied about Hopkins, had anything Casey said about Zenaida been true? Or was Zanny the nanny just a figment of Casey's imagination?

Zanny the Nanny

Casey told investigating officers that she'd last seen Caylee when she dropped her off at Zanny's place at the Sawgrass Apartments in Orlando. Casey had been on her way to work as an event planner at Universal Studios. When she went to pick Caylee up after work, no one was home. She tried calling Zenaida, but Zenaida's telephone had been disconnected. Casey told officers that she sat on the steps of the apartment building and waited for hours, but Zanny never returned to the apartment.

Something about Casey's story wasn't adding up. Casey said she believed her child had been kidnapped, but she hadn't immediately called for help. It took a month for the two-year-old to be reported missing. And even then, it had been Cindy who called 911, not Casey. Casey had never

Casey claimed that she'd spoken to Caylee for a few minutes on the phone on July 15, 2008. But investigators later learned that this was a lie.

told anyone that Caylee was missing, not even her parents or her boyfriend. Instead, Casey claimed that she'd been searching for her daughter on her own. She said she was afraid that if she got the police involved, the kidnapper might harm Caylee.

Casey told detectives that she'd been going to parks and other areas where she thought Zenaida might take Caylee. She said she'd been trying to find information about Zenaida's whereabouts. For Ron Stucker, the chief of criminal investigations at the Orange County Sheriff's Office, and other police officers working on the case, Casey's failure to contact authorities sooner was very frustrating. There was a missing child who needed to be found, and any trail that may have existed had grown cold weeks ago.

As police investigated Caylee's disappearance, Casey's story became even stranger. When police went to the second-floor apartment where Casey said she'd dropped off her daughter, the unit was vacant. But it wasn't vacant

> ### MISSING PERSON REPORTS
>
> Many people believe that a missing person report cannot be filed until 24 hours have passed, but this is a myth. Law enforcement experts say a missing person should be reported to the police immediately. With each minute that a person is missing, it becomes less likely that the person will ever be found. The more time that passes, the more difficult it is for police to find witnesses. And even if witnesses are located, their memories grow less reliable over time.

because Zenaida had fled 31 days earlier, as Casey had said. The unit had actually been empty for many months—far longer than Caylee had been missing. And no one named Zenaida Fernandez-Gonzalez had ever rented a unit in the Sawgrass Apartments building.

After that, Casey said she might have Zenaida's contact information at her place of employment. So she took officers to a Universal Studios office building. When they arrived, Casey's name badge and keycard did not work. They had to be let inside by Universal Studios staff. Casey then led the officers down hallway after hallway, seeming to have forgotten where her office was located. Eventually, she turned to the officers and told them she was not actually a Universal Studios employee

Casey once had a job at Universal Studios. But at the time she led detectives to the office building, she hadn't been working there for years. Casey had been pretending she was still employed.

A FICTITIOUS FRIEND

For several years, George and Cindy believed that Casey was an event planner at Universal Studios. Casey often talked about her job and her friends at work, including a woman named Juliette Lewis who Casey said enjoyed doing volunteer work. Cindy once went to Universal Studios to meet with Lewis and discuss a fundraising event. Cindy said that she waited for Lewis for an hour and a half, but she never arrived. Lewis turned out to be fictitious. No one by that name had ever been an employee of Universal Studios.

and did not have an office. For years, she'd been telling her friends and family that she worked at Universal Studios, but this was not true.

The police thought this was very odd behavior. "Normally in a missing persons investigation, particularly a missing child's investigation, the parent is trying to be helpful," Stucker said. "They want their child to be located."[1] While leading police on a wild goose chase to find Zanny, Casey was wasting valuable time that the police could have spent looking for Caylee. She was not behaving as though she wanted to help them find her child.

Investigating officers soon discovered that not a word Casey had said about Zanny was true. In fact, the babysitter didn't even exist. For nearly two years, Casey had told friends and family that she'd hired Zenaida to work as a nanny. But no one else had ever met the woman. Cindy recalled the many details that Casey had shared with her about Zanny. Casey had said that Zenaida moved from New York to Florida and that she drove a Ford Focus. Casey even shared details

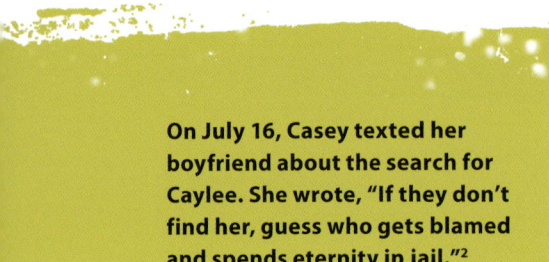

On July 16, Casey texted her boyfriend about the search for Caylee. She wrote, "If they don't find her, guess who gets blamed and spends eternity in jail."[2]

about one of Zanny's haircut appointments with Cindy. But Zenaida Fernandez-Gonzalez was just an elaborate lie. Casey had duped her friends and family, and even the police found her lies to be very convincing at first. As soon as they began to investigate Casey's claims, it became impossible for Casey to keep up the ruse.

Casey Is Charged

Fed up with Casey's lies, the detectives asked to use an empty conference room on the Universal Studios premises to interrogate Casey. Yuri Melich, an experienced detective with the Orange County Sheriff's Department, led the questioning. Up to that point, Casey had been treated like a

ZENAIDA FERNANDEZ-GONZALEZ

Casey claimed that Zenaida "Zanny" Fernandez-Gonzalez had kidnapped Caylee. The police quickly determined that the nanny never existed. However, the name was real. A woman named Zenaida Fernandez-Gonzalez lived in Florida, but she was not a nanny. She was a mother of six and had never met Casey or Caylee Anthony, though she had visited the apartment building where Casey's made-up nanny was said to live and had filled out an information card. Fernandez-Gonzalez said she received death threats, lost her job as a housekeeper, and was evicted from her home after her name was attached to the Anthony case.

Yuri Melich was the lead detective in the Anthony case. He would go on to testify during Casey's trial.

concerned mother. Now, Detective Melich called Casey a liar and demanded to know where Caylee was. Once again, Casey said that she'd left her daughter with Zenaida and didn't know where she was. "This is the honest to God's truth," Casey said.[3]

But Melich wasn't having it. "We already know that you're not telling us the truth," he told Casey. "You know what happened to Caylee—and you know where Caylee is."[4] Using his interrogation skills, Melich continued to try to get the information out of Casey. He told her that he and his fellow officers could look at her as a mother who was just scared. Or they could look at her as "cold, callous and a monster who doesn't care."[5] But even after getting caught in several lies,

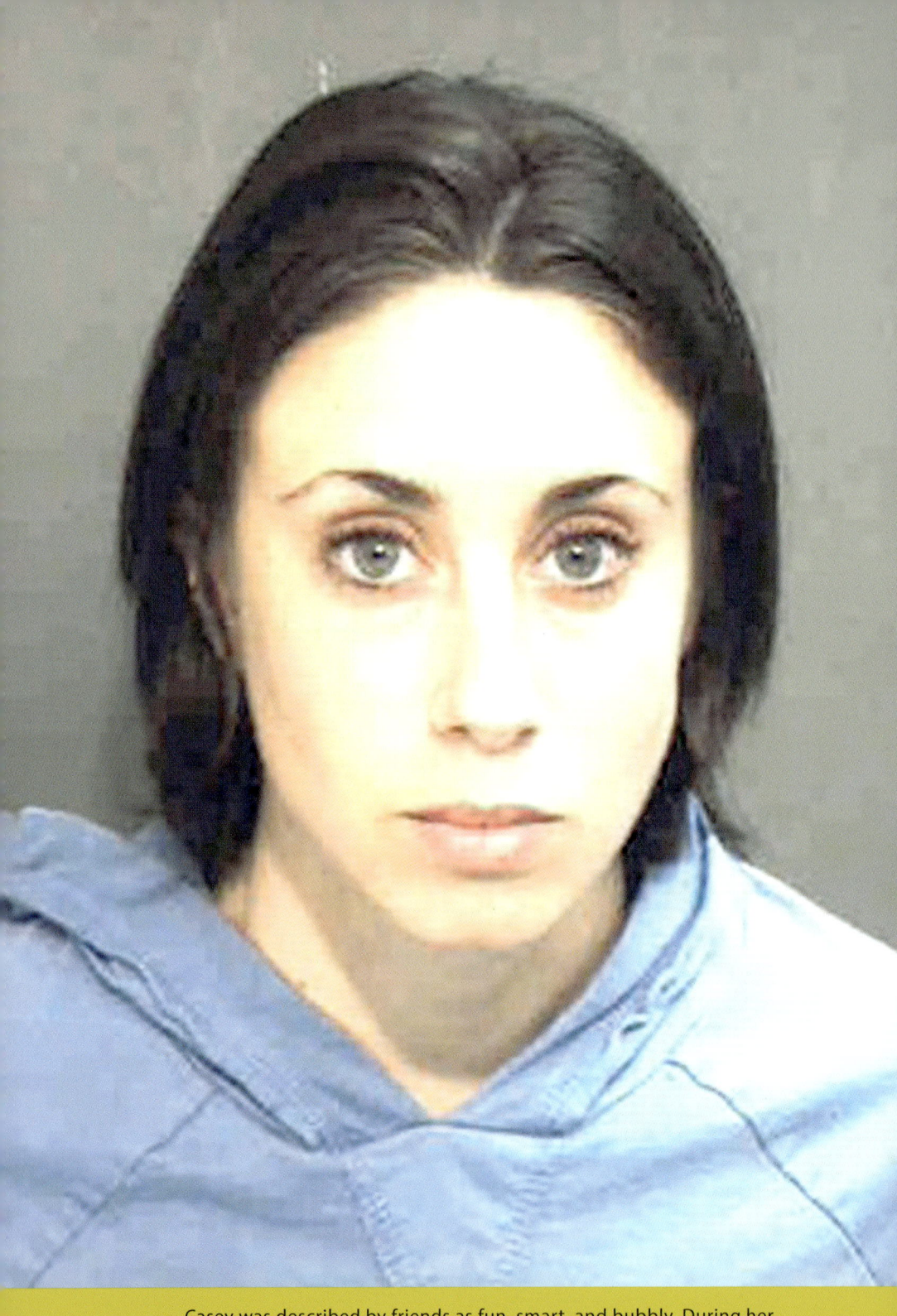

Casey was described by friends as fun, smart, and bubbly. During her arrest and trial, Casey appeared wide-eyed and calm. Spectators noted her pale face and the dark circles under her eyes.

Casey continued to claim that Caylee had been kidnapped by Zanny. She told the investigators that she was "absolutely petrified." "I know my mom will never forgive me," Casey said. "I'm never gonna forgive myself because there's that chance that I might not see Caylee again, and I don't want to think about that."[6] But Melich and the other officers were not convinced.

> On October 14, 2008, Casey's lawyer held a press conference. When asked about Casey's lies and unusual behavior, he responded, "I sincerely believe when we have finally spoken, everyone, and I mean everyone, will sit back and say, now I understand, that explains it."[8]

So, on July 16, 2008, just one day after two-year-old Caylee was reported missing, Casey was arrested and charged with child neglect, providing false information to law enforcement, and interfering with a criminal investigation. Presiding Orange County judge John Jordan ordered that Casey remain in jail without bail. He scolded Casey for not caring more about her missing daughter. He told her, "You left your two-year-old child with a person who does not exist at an apartment you cannot identify, and you lied to your parents about your child's whereabouts."[7]

CHAPTER FOUR

MEDIA FRENZY

On July 17, 2008, one day after Casey's arrest, attorney Jose Baez asked his secretary to check his messages. One of the messages was a call about a prospective client: a 22-year-old woman named Casey Anthony who was being held at the Orange County Jail. Knowing nothing about the case besides the defendant's name, Baez arrived at the jail and informed the guards that he was there to meet with Casey. Baez was surprised to find another lawyer, a public defender, waiting to see Casey too. "This case has been in the news," the lawyer informed Baez, explaining that he'd come to the jail to advise Casey not to talk to anyone without a lawyer present.[1] Unaware of the media storm he was about to step into, Baez met with Casey for the first time.

Two days after signing on to be Casey's lawyer, Baez received messages from national news programs, including *20/20* and *Dateline*. A reporter from *People* magazine came

> Some people criticized Jose Baez for his lack of professional experience and his methods in court. But many also acknowledged that he was a tough lawyer and dedicated advocate for his clients.

directly to Baez's office and waited in the lobby to see him. The entire nation was gripped by the story of the kidnapped toddler in Orlando whose young mother had been arrested for lying to the police. They wanted to hear from the lawyer who'd taken the mother's case.

Cindy and George had been contacted to share their side of the story too. While George wasn't interested in appearing on television, Cindy was happy to have an outlet to talk about Caylee. She was convinced that someone, somewhere, had valuable information that would help the authorities bring her granddaughter home safely. Baez and Cindy traveled together to spread the word about Caylee's disappearance to various news stations. The two of them appeared on several television programs, including the *Today* show.

> ### A FRUSTRATED GRANDMOTHER
>
> Before Caylee's remains were discovered, Cindy was convinced that her granddaughter was still alive. She believed the police should have been looking for Caylee instead of building a case against Casey. "They have not been looking for my granddaughter," Cindy told Meredith Vieira on the *Today* show on October 15, 2008. "I know in my heart that we are going to find Caylee [alive] before this trial takes place."[2]

TV personality Nancy Grace coined the phrase "Tot Mom" as shorthand for referring to Casey Anthony.[3]

An Angry Mob

Casey's bail bond was later set at $500,000.[4] Florida allows defendants to hire someone to post, or pay, their bail for them. This person, called a bail bondsman, charges a fee to post the bail. Leonard Padilla, a bounty hunter from California, worked through a bail bondsman and posted Casey's bail on August 21, 2008. He told *Good Morning America* that he secured Casey's release from jail with the hope that she'd tell him where to find Caylee.

"My theory is this: the mother has lived at home for 22 years. She's a high school dropout. She's got this child. She wanted to start a new life. And then somebody, either a close friend or the father of the child, ended up with the child and they're gone," Padilla said.[5] He added that his goal was to get information out of Casey so that he could find Caylee himself.

Upon Casey's release from jail, she went to live with her parents. With so much attention on the

BAIL BONDS

While waiting for their cases to go to trial, most defendants are allowed to go home. But to give defendants an incentive to return for scheduled court dates, they must post a bail bond. A bail bond is something valuable, such as cash. If the defendant comes back for court, the bail bond is returned. If they miss a court date, the bail bond is forfeited and the defendant goes back to jail. If a person doesn't have enough money, most states allow a defendant to hire a bail bondsman. This person posts the bond on behalf of the defendant for a fee.

During the search for Caylee, the Anthony family hung posters with photos of the missing girl on their front door. One photo showed Caylee resting her head in her hand. This became a widely shared image that made many people interested in the case.

case in the news, many people were already convinced that Casey was guilty. This included many bloggers who decided to organize protests outside of the Anthony home. With the growing popularity of blogging and social media platforms such as Facebook and Twitter, people across the country speculated about whether Casey was guilty. Many people concluded that she was probably involved in her daughter's disappearance. Her freedom made them angry.

Protesters showed up at the Anthony home every day and night to express their anger. Like Padilla, some hoped that Casey's release from jail would lead to answers about Caylee's whereabouts. Padilla theorized that Caylee was alive. The majority of the protesters disagreed. Despite the missing person poster taped to the Anthony family's front door, many people also suspected George and Cindy of helping Casey cover up a crime. One protester said he believed that Casey "was hiding something" and needed to be "confronted until she tells everybody."[6]

Protesters mobbed the street and sidewalk outside of the Anthony house, chanting phrases such as "Baby killer!"[7] Some carried protest signs. One person carried a sign that

During the summer and fall of 2008, protesters and reporters often gathered near the Anthony house. Some believed they could pressure Casey, George, or Cindy into confessing what had happened to Caylee.

said, "My mommy did it!"[8] A dog owner held a sign that said, "I would report my dog missing after 30 seconds, not 30 days."[9] Another woman brought her own toddler to protest with her, giving the child a sign to carry that said, "Would you kill a baby like me?"[10] Some protesters even dressed like demons. George and Cindy put up "No Trespassing" signs and lined their front yard with caution tape, hoping to keep the protesters from getting too close.

One evening, the Anthonys heard a loud banging on their garage door. George and Cindy went to investigate. George wore a T-shirt with a picture of Caylee's face on it. Cindy carried a baseball bat. They opened the garage door and were confronted with several protesters yelling taunts at them. One person grabbed George's T-shirt, pulling him a few steps before Cindy intervened. From within the house, Casey called 911 to report that her parents were being attacked by protesters in the driveway.

Residents in the area called in hundreds of complaints. Orange County sheriff Kevin Beary thought that a police presence was necessary to keep the peace. He stationed patrol cars at each end of the street every day of the week. It cost the Orange County Sheriff's Department nearly $16,000 a month, but Sheriff Beary believed he had no choice. "We have to protect the Anthony (family)," he said. "We [also] have to protect the protesters' rights of free speech."[11]

Over the next few months, the police continued to build their case against Casey. They presented their evidence to an Orange County grand jury. On October 14, 2008, Casey was indicted on new charges—including first-degree murder. This charge involves murder that is intentional and planned. While investigators hadn't found Caylee's remains yet, they were convinced that Casey's story about Caylee getting kidnapped was a lie.

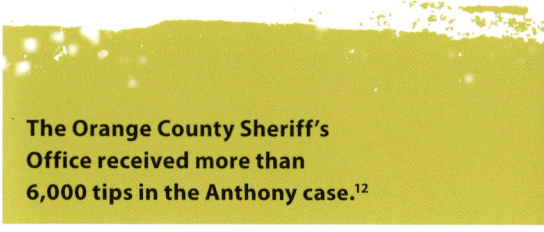

The Orange County Sheriff's Office received more than 6,000 tips in the Anthony case.[12]

They not only believed Caylee was dead but they also thought Casey had killed her. Furthermore, charging Casey with first-degree murder meant that the police and prosecuting attorneys believed there was concrete evidence to prove to a jury that Casey had planned Caylee's murder and followed through with her plan. Casey was back in jail—and if the police and prosecutors got their way, this time she'd remain locked up for the rest of her life.

Kronk Takes a Second Look

On December 11, 2008, Roy Kronk returned to the woods along Suburban Drive. The ground had been wet in August, but it was dry in December. Kronk noticed that the suspicious bag he'd seen over the summer was still there. Deciding to take a closer

> ## NEVER DISTURB A CRIME SCENE
>
> If a person ever comes upon a crime scene, it's important to avoid touching anything. Forensic experts take many photographs and measurements before they touch a single thing. They are also careful to wear appropriate clothing and gloves to protect themselves and any evidence collected at a crime scene. If a crime scene is disturbed, some evidence may be destroyed. For example, footprints and fingerprints may no longer be identifiable if someone else walks through a crime scene or touches evidence. If evidence is tainted, it may be considered unreliable during a trial.

look, he lifted the bag and shook it. That's when he spotted a skull on the ground. Using his meter reader stick, he lifted the skull by one of its eye sockets. Kronk notified his employer immediately, and they contacted the authorities.

Upon hearing that an Orange County meter reader had found skeletal remains, the dispatcher said, "He's not touching this, I hope?"[13] Unfortunately, he had. Later on in the case, attorneys would point this out, arguing that Kronk had tainted the evidence.

This time, crime scene investigators searched the area where Kronk had reported seeing the skull. They recovered dozens of bones that were later determined to be Caylee's remains. Any hope that Caylee would be found alive was now extinguished. Even the homicide detectives, who'd long been convinced of Caylee's death, were deeply affected by the grisly discovery of her remains. Ten years later, Sheriff Beary was

Over the course of ten days, investigators collected more than 390 pieces of evidence from the site where Caylee's remains were found.

still haunted by what they'd found. "I remember my homicide team and my crime scene investigations people crawling in the mud," he recalled, "finding little knuckle bones and little finger bones and what have you. That's something that'll stay with you for the rest of your life."[14]

On December 19, 2008, the bones discovered by Kronk were confirmed to be the skeletal remains of Caylee Anthony.

CHAPTER FIVE

THE TRIAL BEGINS

For the next two years, the prosecution and the defense teams prepared for the trial of the *State of Florida v. Casey Marie Anthony*. They evaluated the evidence, interviewed witnesses, and hired experts. Meanwhile, Casey remained in jail, wondering if she'd ever know freedom again. She'd been indicted on the charges of murder in the first degree, aggravated child abuse, aggravated manslaughter, and multiple counts of providing false information. With all of these charges, there was a possibility that Casey would spend the rest of her life in prison—or worse. Prosecutors were seeking the harshest possible penalty under Florida law: death.

In early May 2011, jury selection for the trial began. The presiding judge in the case was Belvin Perry Jr. Given the level of media attention the case had received, Judge Perry knew

While preparing for the trial, several attorneys joined Casey's defense team. This included Dorothy Clay Sims, *left*, and Cheney Mason, *right*.

it would be difficult to find an impartial jury panel. "I'm not naïve enough to think we'll encounter no one who has heard of this case," he said, "but the goal is to find people who have not been oversaturated with media."[1]

In addition to finding jurors who hadn't prejudged the facts of the case, the authorities needed to find jurors who did not have strong opinions about the death penalty. It was also necessary to select jurors who could physically, emotionally, and financially endure the hardship of a six-to-eight-week trial. In a case with so much media spectacle surrounding it, jurors would have to be sequestered. This meant

> **In Florida, if a killing was planned, the charge is murder in the first degree. But if a killing happened in the heat of the moment, the charge is manslaughter.**

RECUSAL OF JUDGE STRICKLAND

Judge Stan Strickland was originally assigned to preside over the Anthony case. But he recused himself in August 2010 because of comments he made to David Knechel, a true crime blogger known as Marinade Dave. Spotting Knechel in the courtroom's gallery, Judge Strickland summoned him to the bench for a friendly chat. He complimented Knechel's coverage of the Anthony case as being "fair and civilized." Casey's team took issue with this description since Knechel had posted negative comments about Casey on his blog, including "Guilty as charged" and "Casey Anthony must die!"[2] After Judge Strickland stepped down, Judge Belvin Perry Jr. replaced him.

that for more than a month, the jurors would be separated from their loved ones and unable to go to work. They would have no access to cell phones or the internet either. Phone calls would have to be made from a landline and supervised. Family members would be allowed to visit with jurors only on weekends, and the jurors would be forbidden from discussing the case.

Casey's defense team filed a motion for a change of venue, asking that the trial be held somewhere outside of Orlando because it would be difficult to find local jurors who were unfamiliar with the case. Judge Perry denied the motion to change the trial venue.

> **In his 2012 book *Presumed Guilty*, defense attorney Jose Baez wrote that he was satisfied with the jury selection in the Anthony trial.**

However, he did agree that finding an impartial Orlando jury would be impossible. Because of this, Judge Perry made the unconventional decision to bring in jurors from another county in Florida. Jury selection took place in Clearwater, Florida, which was located approximately 100 miles (160 km) away from Orlando.[3] During the jury selection process, both prosecutors and defense counsel interviewed potential jurors to determine whether they could be fair during the trial. Once all the jury members had been selected, they were transported to Orlando. There, the jurors would stay in a hotel for the trial's duration.

The jury selected for the Anthony trial was made up of seven men and five women, ranging from ages 32 to 65. It included a nurse, a teacher, and a salesman. Several of the jurors were parents.

Opening Statements Begin

At 9:00 a.m. on May 24, 2011, lead prosecutor Linda Drane Burdick stood before the jury, ready to give the state's opening argument. With the calm, controlled voice of an experienced prosecutor, she told the jury they'd heard all about the defendant, Casey, throughout the jury selection process. But now there was another person whose story needed to be told.

"It is time to tell the story of a little girl named Caylee," Burdick said.[4]

Burdick appealed to the jurors' emotions, presenting a day-by-day account of Casey's activities during the month her daughter was missing. Throughout this account of Casey's comings and goings, Burdick continued to repeat one question: "Where is Caylee Marie Anthony?"[5] She showed the jury photographs of Caylee, a happy girl who loved to sing and dance, followed by photographs of the two-year-old's skeletal remains.

Burdick laid out the circumstantial evidence that the jury would hear throughout the trial. Over the course of the next six to eight weeks, jurors would hear testimony from dozens of witnesses and experts. There would be testimony about Casey's car, which prosecutors believed was used to transport Caylee's dead body. Burdick told the jury it would also hear evidence from crime scene investigators who collected Caylee's bones.

CONTEMPT OF COURT

Judge Perry had a zero-tolerance policy for anyone who violated his court order prohibiting talk of the case. A 29-year-old woman named Elisabeth Rogers wandered into the courtroom while jury selection was taking place. She shouted, "She killed somebody anyway!" Perry held Rogers in contempt of court and sentenced her to serve two days in jail.[6] Juror 3207, 35-year-old Jonathan Green, approached a reporter during a recess hoping it would get him out of jury duty. He was chastised by the judge, held in contempt, and ordered to pay $450.[7] But Green also got his wish—he was dismissed from jury duty.

> ### JOSE BAEZ
>
> Jose Angel Baez is a US Navy veteran and one of the nation's best-known attorneys. After rising to fame as Casey Anthony's lead defense attorney, Baez went on to represent several high-profile clients, including former New England Patriots player Aaron Hernandez. Baez is a faculty member at Harvard Law School, where he teaches trial advocacy and techniques. In 2022, the National Trial Lawyers Association named him Criminal Defense Trial Lawyer of the Year. Baez is also a *New York Times* best-selling author.

It would hear about the alleged murder weapon: duct tape used to suffocate Caylee. And Burdick made sure the jury knew the prosecution's theory about Casey's motive for killing her daughter. "Caylee's death allowed Casey Anthony to live the good life—at least for those 31 days," Burdick said, referring to the time before Caylee was reported missing. "At the end of this case you will have no trouble concluding that Caylee Anthony was murdered by her mother, Casey Anthony."[8]

A Tragic Accident?

When it was the defense team's turn to provide opening arguments, attorney Jose Baez shocked prosecutors, spectators in the courtroom, and the public with several bombshells. He said that Caylee hadn't been murdered. And she hadn't been kidnapped. In fact, she was never missing at all. On June 16, 2008, she'd drowned in Cindy and George's above-ground swimming pool.

Burdick was an experienced prosecutor known for her aggressive questioning methods. Before the Anthony trial, she had worked on several high-profile homicide and child abuse cases.

According to Baez, Casey and George were the only adults home at the time, and they panicked. George screamed at Casey, "Look what you've done! Your mother will never forgive you! You will go to jail for child neglect for the rest of your life!"[9] Then, according to the defense's opening statement, George covered up Caylee's death and disposed of her body.

So why did Casey concoct an elaborate lie about a kidnapping if Caylee's death was really an accidental drowning?

During his opening statement, Baez used posters and photos that showed the Anthony family's house and swimming pool. He argued that the pool ladder hadn't been pulled up, which allowed Caylee to get into the pool by herself.

Baez told the jury that lying was a skill Casey had picked up at an early age because of sexual abuse by her father. He explained that when Casey was only 13 years old, she would be sexually abused by her father and "then go to school and play as if nothing was wrong."[10]

This history of sexual abuse and hiding family secrets was also why Casey had lived her life as though nothing was wrong during the month before she told anyone Caylee was missing. As Baez detailed Casey's history of sexual abuse for the jury, Casey buried her face in her hands and sobbed. "This is not a murder case. This is not a manslaughter case," Baez said. "This is a tragic accident that happened to some very disturbed people."[11]

CHAPTER SIX

WHITE PONTIAC SUNFIRE

Home to major tourist destinations such as Walt Disney World and Universal Studios, Orlando is known as the theme park capital of the world. But in the summer of 2011, many people were more interested in getting tickets to Casey Anthony's murder trial. The trial was televised. Countless news programs, crime bloggers, and social media posts presented play-by-plays of every minute of the court proceedings.

Millions of people tuned in on their televisions, computers, and cell phones. But for some people, watching the trial on a screen wasn't good enough. They wanted to be inside the courtroom to witness it firsthand. With only around 50 seats available daily, tickets to the trial became a precious commodity and were handed out each morning at the courthouse.[1]

Dozens of people waited in line for hours to get tickets to the Anthony trial. Police officers monitored the line to prevent people from fighting or stampeding.

A COSTLY HAND GESTURE

During the trial, Judge Perry expected everyone present to be on their best behavior. This included both lawyers and spectators. So when spectator Matthew Bartlett, a 28-year-old restaurant server, made a rude hand gesture to prosecutor Jeff Ashton, Perry was furious. He told Bartlett that if the jury had seen him extending his middle finger at Ashton's back, it could have jeopardized the entire trial. Perry held Bartlett in contempt of court, sentencing him to six days in jail, a $400 fine, and $223 in court costs.[2]

People camped out overnight hoping to receive a ticket.

It wasn't always a peaceful crowd. People fought over their positions in the ticket line. Cutting in line was met with anger and sometimes violence from the crowd. But having a line didn't work very well, anyway. Since no one was allowed on the courthouse property until the doors opened, the crowd gathered across the street. As soon as the courthouse doors opened, the line disappeared as people rushed forward to try to get a ticket. One morning, a woman fell during the mad dash to the door and had to be treated by paramedics. A few people stopped to help her. But most people ran over her or past her, focused solely on getting a ticket to the trial.

"It is a mad stampede of angry people," said 22-year-old Walt Disney World worker Natalie Sutton. She'd arrived at 3:15 a.m. to get a spot near the front of the line, and she attended multiple days of the trial. She loved hearing the

The trial took place in Courtroom 23 on the twenty-third floor of the Orange County Courthouse. Reporters and spectators had to follow specific rules while inside the courtroom.

testimony from the forensic experts and found the science to be fascinating. Polly Wilson, a 42-year-old teacher, agreed. She described seeing the trial in person as "riveting—better than on TV."[3]

Kathi Jennings had also taken an interest in the Anthony case and wanted to watch it inside the courtroom. After witnessing the ticket stampede firsthand, Jennings realized that there needed to be a more orderly system for getting a ticket than attempting to form a line across the street. So the next night, she brought along a Sharpie marker. As people arrived, she wrote their number in line onto their hand. The first ten people arrived before 2:00 a.m., and it didn't take long before all 50 seats were claimed. People nicknamed Jennings the "Sharpie Lady," and she started wearing a T-shirt with those words emblazoned across the chest.[4]

Her system worked well—until it didn't. Before long, people objected to her method. Others tried to establish their own rules. A "Sharpie Lady" imposter even came along. When the situation came to a boiling point, resulting in punches being thrown, officials decided to change the process for receiving tickets. For the remaining weeks of the trial, a lottery system was put in place. Hopeful spectators would be required to get in line at 4:00 p.m. to receive a ticket for the following day's proceedings. The next morning, they'd discover if their ticket number was granted a seat inside the courtroom to witness the trial in person.

A Terrible Smell

Much of the testimony that captivated spectators focused on the white Pontiac Sunfire. Both the prosecution and the defense agreed that the car smelled bad after being abandoned in a parking lot and towed to an impound lot. But the prosecution and the defense had different theories about the source of the odor.

The car had been abandoned for three weeks at the height of summer before George and Cindy received notice that it had been impounded. The car was registered to them, but they'd given the car to Casey to use as her personal vehicle. When George opened the car doors at the impound lot, a strong odor wafted out of the car. He determined that the smell was coming from the car's trunk.

> ### TYPES OF EVIDENCE
>
> During a trial, different types of evidence may be presented to the jury. Direct evidence proves a fact without requiring jurors to make inferences. For example, if a defendant admits that they committed a crime, a jury does not need to draw conclusions about what happened. They need to decide only whether they believe the defendant's confession. Circumstantial evidence, on the other hand, does not provide direct proof. For example, a witness who sees the defendant running from the crime scene can't say for sure that the defendant committed the crime. In a case like this, jurors need to weigh all the evidence and make inferences about the defendant's guilt or innocence.

At the trial, George testified that he was afraid to open the trunk. He said the smell was so terrible that he feared his daughter or granddaughter, whom he hadn't seen in a few weeks, might be inside. As a former police officer, George had some experience with the smell of human decomposition. When the trunk was opened, he was immensely relieved to find only a bag of garbage. An employee at the impound lot, Simon Birch, removed the bag of trash and threw it away.

The stench was so bad that George drove the vehicle home with the windows rolled down. During cross-examination, Casey's attorney asked George why he didn't call the police immediately if he believed the car smelled like a dead body had been inside it. "I didn't want to believe what I was smelling," George replied.[5]

Birch also testified about the car's stench, agreeing that it smelled like a rotting corpse. He'd been exposed to the smell of decomposition in a vehicle before and thought the Sunfire had a similar odor. But like George, Birch didn't report the smell to anyone.

The prosecution theorized that Casey had stored and transported Caylee's corpse in the trunk of the Sunfire.

Cindy and George were both questioned as witnesses. At one point, Cindy broke down in tears while testifying about her 911 calls and the odor in Casey's car.

To support their argument, they called Dr. Arpad Vass to testify regarding the "smell of death" in the car.[6] Dr. Vass was a forensic anthropologist and research scientist at the Oak Ridge National Laboratory in Tennessee. He'd studied human decomposition for 20 years.[7]

> The bodies used for decomposition research at the Forensic Anthropology Center are donated. People can make arrangements to have their bodies donated to the center after they die.

As part of his research, Dr. Vass utilized the Forensic Anthropology Center at the University of Tennessee. More commonly referred to as the Body Farm, the Forensic Anthropology Center offers researchers the opportunity to study human bodies as they decompose. Some of the bodies are buried, others are left on the surface of the ground, and some are enclosed in vehicles or other containers.

The prosecution presented Dr. Vass as an odor analysis expert. Odor analysis to detect the smell of human decomposition had never been used in a US court of law before. Judge Perry's decision to allow it was controversial since it was experimental and relatively new. Some legal analysts thought it was foolish for the prosecution to use Dr. Vass as an expert witness. Greta Van Susteren, a lawyer and news anchor, said, "[T]he dumbest idea the prosecution could do was put that witness on. He's sort of a novel expert, a smell expert, an

63

Prosecutor Jeff Ashton, *left*, discussed air samples with Dr. Vass, *right*, during the trial. The samples were kept in metal evidence cans.

odor expert, and why in the world did the prosecution do that? They're so over-trying the case."[8]

Using air samples collected from a piece of carpet in the vehicle's trunk, Dr. Vass tested for certain chemicals believed to be present when a body is decomposing. He told the jury

that when he first opened the can containing the air sample, he was "shocked that that little bitty can could have that much odor." One of the chemicals he found in the air sample was chloroform. Dr. Vass testified that he found a "shockingly high" amount of chloroform in his analysis. While chloroform is normally present in decomposition, this was an "unusually high" amount, according to Dr. Vass.⁹ The prosecution used his findings to conclude that Casey had poisoned Caylee with chloroform, using it to put her to sleep before murdering her.

Evidence collected from the Anthony family's home computer seemed to support the prosecution's theory. The Google search history on the computer included searches for the word "chloroform," along with terms such as "neck breaking" and "household weapons."¹⁰ These searches were made in March 2008. The prosecution said the searches suggested that Casey had planned her daughter's murder.

> **Cindy Anthony left prosecutors baffled when she testified that she was the one who had googled "chloroform." She said she had been trying to google "chlorophyll."¹¹ But Cindy was at work on the day the searches were made from the Anthony home.**

However, Dr. Vass's testimony conflicted with that of other witnesses. One was forensic chemist Michael Sigman. He also studied air samples collected from the Sunfire. While Sigman found chloroform to be present, he determined that the amount was very low. According to his findings, gasoline was the main component identified in the sample.

Another witness for the prosecution, FBI forensic chemist Michael Rickenbach, had similar findings. Rickenbach testified that he found only low amounts of chloroform, equal to the amount found in cleaning supplies. In some of his testing, he found no chloroform at all.

A Single Hair

Investigators found a single nine-inch (23 cm) strand of brown hair in the trunk of the Pontiac Sunfire.[12] The state's expert was Karen Korsberg Lowe, an FBI detective who specializes in studying hair samples. She testified that the hair may have belonged to Caylee. It was similar in appearance to a hair she'd examined from the girl's hairbrush. DNA testing linked the strand of hair to Caylee's maternal line, meaning the hair could have come from Caylee or several of her relatives, including her mother, grandmother, great-grandmother, and uncle. Lowe testified that since the hair did not have tissue attached to it, it was impossible to get a more precise DNA match.

When Lowe examined the hair under a microscope, she noticed a dark band circling the

SOIL SAMPLES

FBI geologist Maureen Bottrell collected pairs of shoes from the Anthony home to test them against soil samples retrieved from the site where Caylee's bones were recovered. Of the 22 pairs of shoes that were tested, only three had enough soil to perform the necessary tests.[13] None of the soil in the treads of the shoes matched the area where Caylee's remains were recovered. On cross-examination, Bottrell conceded that she could not conclude whether Casey had worn the shoes at the scene. She could only say there was no soil on the shoes that matched soil from the recovery site.

root which was "consistent with apparent decomposition."[14] FBI forensic analyst Stephen Shaw, another hair expert, provided witness testimony as well. He agreed with Lowe that root-banding is often found in hair plucked from the head of a corpse. But he said he could not testify that root-banding is present only in dead bodies. Neither expert could say with certainty how long the hair had been in the trunk of the car or whether it had come from Caylee's head.

Bugs

The prosecution also hired Dr. Neal Haskell, who was a forensic entomologist. He testified that he'd found maggots on a paper towel inside the trash bag that had been left in Casey's car. Dr. Haskell said it was possible that the paper towel had been used to wipe up fluids from Caylee's decomposing body.

The defense hired Dr. Timothy Huntington, a forensic entomologist and assistant professor of biology from Concordia University, to conduct his own review of the evidence. He testified that it's normal to find maggots inside weeks-old garbage. Dr. Huntington had also performed extensive research on

FBI serologist Heather Seubert examined the white Pontiac Sunfire's trunk. Serologists study blood and other bodily fluids. Seubert found no DNA or blood in the trunk.

Blowflies are attracted to rotting trash and flesh. The presence of these bugs can help forensic experts learn more about a person's time of death.

the decomposition of bodies left inside closed car trunks. He used dead pigs in place of humans in his research. He testified that the absence of hundreds, or even thousands, of blowflies inside the trunk indicated that it had never held a corpse. According to Dr. Huntington, if there had been human decomposition in the vehicle, there would have been significantly more bugs present than the amount found inside the garbage bag.

CHAPTER SEVEN

HOMICIDE BY UNDETERMINED MEANS

When Caylee's skeletonized remains were discovered in December 2008, medical examiner Dr. Jan Garavaglia examined the bones. With nothing but dry bones remaining, it was very difficult—if not impossible—to discern the cause of death. Sometimes trauma to the bones can help investigators figure out a victim's cause of death. But in Caylee's case, her bones showed no signs of trauma. Nevertheless, Dr. Garavaglia listed the cause of death to be "homicide by undetermined means."[1] During the trial in 2011, this determination was the prosecution's greatest hurdle. Could they prove Caylee had been murdered without being able to say how she'd died?

But Dr. Garavaglia was confident in her findings. At the trial, she was a star witness for the prosecution—literally.

Forensics experts testified about the duct tape found on Caylee's skull. One investigator found the outline of a heart on the tape. It matched the shape of heart-shaped stickers found in the Anthony home.

As the host of her own cable television show on the Discovery Health Channel, *Dr. G: Medical Examiner*, Dr. Garavaglia didn't shy away from the spotlight. She explained her findings to the jury in a clear, commanding voice. She admitted that she couldn't tell from Caylee's bones how the girl had died, so she looked at the surrounding circumstances from the police investigation.

The fact that Caylee's body had been discarded in the woods, combined with the fact that Casey had not reported Caylee missing for a month, were two of the main factors that led to her homicide conclusion. "We know by our observations," Dr. Garavaglia said, "that it's a red flag when a child has not been reported to authorities."[2] The third factor was a piece of duct tape found near Caylee's skull.

Possible Murder Weapon

Caylee's bones were found scattered in the woods along with trash and other debris. Bits of a Winnie the Pooh blanket were found, as well. A strip of duct tape was hanging from Caylee's skull. Since the piece of duct tape was large enough to cover a girl's nose and mouth to suffocate her, investigators believed the tape could be the murder weapon. Two additional strips of duct tape were found several feet away from Caylee's skull.

When defense attorney Cheney Mason cross-examined Dr. Garavaglia during the trial, the doctor refused to concede that Caylee's death could have been an accident, despite having no medical evidence to the contrary. Skeptical, Mason said, "You're trying to tell this jury 100 percent that this death couldn't be an accident?" Dr. Garavaglia doubled down, saying, "Accidental deaths are reported 100 percent of the time—unless there's a reason not to."[3] Her mind was set, and she stuck to her conclusion that Caylee's death was a homicide.

Mason also questioned meter reader Roy Kronk at the trial. Kronk admitted that he'd stuck his meter reader stick into

After hearing testimony about Caylee's bones and seeing graphic photos of her remains, Casey appeared shaken. She was seen crying, resting her head in her hands, and looking away from the photos.

the eye socket of Caylee's skull to move it for a better look. By moving the skull, Kronk tainted the crime scene. He wasn't the only one to disturb Caylee's bones at the site, though. Forensic anthropologist Dr. John Schultz provided testimony about animals gnawing on and moving Caylee's bones. Casey became visibly upset and physically ill during Schultz's testimony, so Judge Perry canceled the court proceedings for the remainder of the day.

The defense team hired Dr. Werner Spitz to examine Caylee's skeletal remains. Dr. Spitz was a world-renowned forensic pathologist, a kind of doctor who specializes in performing autopsies and determining cause of death. He pointed out that there was no DNA evidence discovered at the site to tie Casey to Caylee's body. The strip of duct tape that prosecutors believed to be the murder weapon also contained no DNA or fingerprints. In Dr. Spitz's opinion, this meant the tape

THE MEDICAL DETECTIVE

Dr. Werner Spitz enjoys his work, likening it to being a "medical detective."[4] He examines human remains to find answers. With thousands of autopsies under his belt, Dr. Spitz has worked on some of history's biggest cases, including the assassination of President John F. Kennedy, the assassination of civil rights activist Martin Luther King Jr., and the O. J. Simpson murder trial. He has been hired regularly by both defendants and prosecutors to provide expert testimony in court. In a 2022 interview with *Time*, Dr. Spitz said he had no plans to retire.

Werner Spitz used a model of a human skull during his testimony. He believed the duct tape had been placed on Caylee's skull to hold the lower jawbone of the skull in place.

must have become affixed to the skull after decomposition had occurred. Otherwise, Caylee's skin cells and fluids from decomposition would have been present on the sticky side of the tape. Dr. Spitz said it was possible that when Kronk or wild animals tainted the crime scene, the tape was introduced to Caylee's skull.

Additionally, Dr. Spitz testified that Dr. Garavaglia's work had been "shoddy" since she had not opened Caylee's skull to conduct a thorough autopsy. In his opinion, a full autopsy should have been completed before declaring the cause of death. "The skull, the head, is part of the body," Dr. Spitz said, "and when you do an autopsy you examine the whole body."[5]

Closing Arguments

The closing arguments of the trial began on July 3, 2011. Prosecutor Jeff Ashton began the state of Florida's closing argument by showing a video of Casey playing with Caylee. In the video, the mother and daughter laughed gleefully as they played together on the floor. After the video ended, Ashton said, "It's easy to be a parent when you're playing with your children. It's easy to be a parent when children are a joy."[6] But then he talked about the responsibilities and sacrifices of parenthood, which he said became too much for Casey to handle.

He painted a picture of Casey as a selfish young woman who wanted a carefree life. He walked the jury through the evidence again, including the month that Casey spent going to bars and a tattoo parlor while Caylee's body was decomposing in the woods. He appealed to the jurors' sense of decency and morality while reminding them of Casey's lies.

Casey's text messages and social media posts were used as evidence against her during the trial. On July 7, 2008, for example, she posted a poem on her MySpace profile. It read, "What is given can be taken away. Everyone lies, everyone dies."[7]

When it was the defense's turn to address the jury, Baez acknowledged that the prosecution had done a good job of appealing to everyone's emotions. But he explained to the jurors that they were required to make their decision based on the evidence, not on their feelings.

Baez pointed out that Florida's courtroom guidelines specifically instruct jurors not to base a verdict on whether they feel upset with someone. He admitted that his biggest fear was that the jury would convict Casey because they were angry with her. Baez urged them to instead hold the prosecution to a high standard of evidence. He said they'd failed to answer the one question that mattered: "How did Caylee die?"[8]

Baez contended that if the jurors couldn't answer that question, then reasonable doubt existed, and they must find Casey not guilty of manslaughter or murder in the first degree. Baez reiterated that Casey did not kill her daughter. He said

> **THE CSI EFFECT**
>
> With the popularity of crime-related television shows, jurors have become less likely to convict defendants without direct evidence or ironclad forensic evidence. This is called the CSI effect. In the popular TV show *CSI*, crime scene investigators solve crimes quickly and efficiently. They often use forensic science to find DNA evidence, which then leads to the defendant's confession. But in cases such as Anthony's, where there is no blood or DNA evidence, no eyewitnesses, and no confession, the CSI effect may play a role. This can make it more difficult for prosecutors to secure a conviction.

Casey's defense team showed the jury photos of Caylee climbing the pool ladder. In the photos, she is wearing a life jacket and is supported from behind by her grandmother Cindy.

Caylee's death was an accidental drowning that George Anthony covered up. Baez also showed the jury photographs of Caylee opening the sliding glass door at the Anthony house on her own and climbing the ladder to the pool. With a few photographs, he showed the jury that Caylee could have accidentally drowned in the pool.

In Florida, the State's attorneys are given the opportunity to address the jury one more time after the defense gives its closing argument. Once again, the prosecution played on the emotions of the jury. Burdick asked the jury who stood to benefit from Caylee's death. As the jurors mulled over the question in their minds, Burdick displayed a picture of Casey's "Bella Vita" tattoo. "There's your answer," she told them.[9]

> ## BURDEN OF PROOF
>
> Casey opted not to testify at her jury trial. The media remarked on this decision, but it's common for defendants to remain silent at their trials. In a criminal case, the state bears the burden of proof. This means they must prove to every member of the jury that the defendant is guilty beyond a reasonable doubt. Defendants don't have to prove their innocence. They aren't required to testify, present evidence, or question any witnesses at all.

CHAPTER EIGHT

THE VERDICTS

The 12 members of the jury deliberated for less than 11 hours before finalizing their verdicts on July 5, 2011.[1] They did not ask to review any of the evidence before coming to a unanimous verdict on each count of the indictment. As the jury members filed into the courtroom, Baez studied their faces. Their expressions were stony, and none of them made eye contact with him. Baez couldn't tell if that was a good or bad thing for his client. In that moment, he couldn't read the jurors at all.

One of the jury members, a physical education teacher who'd taken lots of notes during the trial, handed over the jury's verdict forms. Judge Perry read through the verdicts twice before handing the papers to the clerk. Casey stood next to Baez as the clerk read each verdict, beginning with the most serious count. "As to the charge of first-degree murder, verdict as to count one," the clerk read, "we the jury find the defendant

Casey appeared scared and pale as she waited to hear the verdicts. As the verdicts were read, she cried and held hands with her attorneys Baez and Sims.

not guilty, so say we all."² Casey's face crumpled with emotion as tears sprang to her eyes.

The clerk continued to read the verdicts. The jury had also found Casey to be not guilty of aggravated manslaughter and aggravated child abuse. They did, however, find her guilty of all four counts of providing false information to law enforcement. Judge Perry sentenced Casey to the maximum sentence allowed by the law. Since she was convicted only of misdemeanors, he could sentence her to only one year in jail on each count, to be served back-to-back, for a total of four years. Casey would also have to pay a $1,000 fine for each count. With credit for the time she'd already been incarcerated, as well as credit for good behavior, Casey would be released from jail less than two weeks after the verdicts were read.³

Prosecutor Jeff Ashton was utterly shocked.

CHENEY MASON REMEMBERS

Cheney Mason was a senior lawyer on Casey's defense team. In a CNN interview ten years after Caylee's disappearance, Mason recalled the first time he saw Casey. "She did not look like any kind of monster. She looked like a scared little young girl. . . . [M]y intuitive feelings were that she was not guilty of doing it," he said. Mason had viewed photographs and videos of Casey and Caylee together, seeing a loving mother and child. He was determined to keep the state from sentencing Casey to death. A decade later, Mason's feelings hadn't changed. "I'm never going to believe that [she killed her daughter]," he said.⁴

THE ANTHONY TRIAL BY THE NUMBERS

- There were **12 jurors** in the Anthony trial, **7 women** and **5 men**.
- Casey was indicted on **7 counts**, including **3 felonies** and **4 misdemeanors**.
- The trial included **33 days** of testimony.
- **91 witnesses** were questioned during the trial.
- **More than 400 pieces of evidence** were presented during the trial.
- The jury deliberated for **11 hours**.
- Casey was convicted of **4 misdemeanors**. **2 convictions** were overturned on appeal.

The Anthony trial was one of the most highly publicized trials in the country. It lasted about six weeks. During that time, millions of people tuned in to hear the testimony and evidence.

He later detailed his feelings about the verdicts in his book, *Imperfect Justice: Prosecuting Casey Anthony*. He wrote, "It might be egotistical, but it never occurred to me that all twelve of those jurors, in that amount of time, could have rejected all that evidence."[5]

Baez's reaction to the verdicts was much different from Ashton's. Prosecutors were seeking the death penalty for Casey, but she'd walked away with only a few misdemeanors on her record. At the press conference following the reading of the verdicts, Baez was proud to say he saved a life. Despite his happiness for his client, he was quick to point out that there were no winners. The death of two-year-old Caylee was a tragedy, and she'd died far too young.

Public Outrage

The jury's decision was met with public outrage. After being sequestered for nearly two months, the jurors didn't realize how much the Anthony case had been followed by the rest of the world. They faced scorn, ridicule, and even death threats. Just outside the courthouse, protesters waved signs that said things such as "Juror 1–12, Guilty of Murder!!!!," "No Guts Jury," and "No Justice for Caylee!"[6] A Skyline Chili restaurant even posted a sign that read, "Pinellas County jurors NOT Welcome!"[7] Many people expressed their dismay about the verdict in social media posts.

After the verdict was announced, many people gathered outside the courthouse to protest the jury's decision.

Celebrities criticized the jury too. TV personality Nancy Grace called the jurors "kooky."[8] Reality TV star Kim Kardashian tweeted, "WHAT!!!!???!!!! CASEY ANTHONY FOUND NOT GUILTY!!!! I am speechless!!!"[9] Actress Vivica A. Fox tweeted, "My heart is ripped apart! How dare those idiots on that Jury not see the truth?"[10]

Forensic psychiatrist Dr. Carole Lieberman believed there was so much public outcry over the case because "the media convicted Casey before the jury decided on the verdict." She said, "It's hard for people to accept an outcome that is different than what they already decided, even though there wasn't enough evidence brought up to show that."[11] People had been captivated by the case, and they wanted justice for Caylee.

In Florida, the names of jurors are typically released immediately following a trial. But Judge Perry feared that the jurors would be in danger if their identities were discovered while tempers were running so hot. "People have no reservation . . . about walking up to an individual, pulling a gun or knife . . . and because they disagree with them, hurt them or kill them," he said.[12]

To protect the jurors, Perry decided to implement a three-month cooldown period. This meant he would wait for three months before making the jurors' names available to the public. This gave the jurors time to settle back into their lives without being immediately thrust into the public eye. It would

> ## JUSTICE IS SERVED
>
> In a CNN interview, Judge Perry admitted that he was surprised by the outcome of Casey's trial. Though the state's evidence was all circumstantial, he'd thought "there was a high probability that [Casey] would be found guilty of some form of homicide." But this group of jurors needed to know how Caylee died, and the prosecution couldn't give them the answer. Regardless of how anyone else felt about the jury's decision, Perry pointed out that "when a case goes through the process that we have all agreed to live by, then justice is served."[13]

also give the public time to calm down and shift their attention to other matters.

The Jurors Speak

When the jurors started to speak publicly about their deliberations, one thing became immediately clear: they didn't like Casey any more than the public did. The jurors' decision came down to the prosecution not meeting its burden of proof beyond a reasonable doubt. The prosecution couldn't say how Caylee had died. The only thing the jurors knew for sure was that Casey was a liar, so that's all they could find her guilty of.

But this wasn't a decision the jury came to lightly. One juror described the tense atmosphere in the deliberation room when the jurors realized

> After the trial, one of the jurors told *People* magazine that the jury liked Baez better than the prosecutors.

the magnitude of their decision. The juror said, "[W]e sat there for a few minutes and were like, 'Holy crap, we are letting her go free.... But what else can we do? We promised to follow the law.'"[14]

None of the jurors spoke to the media on the day the verdicts were read. Juror #3, 32-year-old nursing student Jennifer Ford, later told ABC News this was because "we were sick to our stomach to get that verdict." After six weeks of sitting through the trial, Ford said, "I have no idea what happened to that child."[15]

Juror #2, a 46-year-old man with a wife and two kids, felt the same way. In an interview with the *St. Petersburg Times*, he said, "I just swear to God . . . I wish we had more evidence to put her away, I truly do. But it wasn't there."[16]

The fact that the prosecution was seeking the death penalty factored into the jury's decision. Ford told *Good Morning America*, "If they charged her with other things, we probably could have gotten a guilty verdict, absolutely. But not for death, not for first-degree murder. That's a very substantial charge."[17] Ford clarified her feelings further to ABC News, saying, "If they want to charge and they want me to take someone's life, they have to prove it. They have to prove it, or else I'm a murderer too."[18]

An Exit Strategy

Casey's release from jail posed a problem. She was universally hated, with many people wishing her harm. With her life in danger, she couldn't just walk out of jail. A SWAT team in full riot gear would make sure she got safely out of the jail and into a vehicle. But after that, Casey would be on her own. Her defense team devised a way to get her to safety.

News crews in helicopters hovered overhead, waiting to follow Casey once she left the jail. Protesters were also waiting outside. Escorted by the SWAT team, Baez walked Casey out of the jail and into a waiting vehicle. Baez instructed the driver to pull into a nearby parking garage, where multiple vehicles with taped-up windows were waiting. Baez and Casey quickly jumped into a different vehicle and left the garage along with the decoy cars.

> ### IMPACT ON THE JURY
>
> Studies have shown that as many as 50 percent of jurors experience trauma and stress-related symptoms. Many struggle with depression and post-traumatic stress disorder following a trial. This is especially true in cases involving violent crimes and graphic evidence. Cases involving the death penalty and jury sequestration increase stress too. The jurors in the Anthony trial endured all these factors. One juror spoke anonymously to *People* magazine in 2021. The juror said they think about the Anthony case at least once every day.

Each car headed in a different direction. The helicopters were forced to follow different cars. Casey and Baez headed to a nearby airport, where a small plane was waiting.

Baez and Casey boarded the small plane and flew to St. George Island, Florida. Casey's defense team had rented a beachfront property to help Casey hide from the media and plan her next steps. On her first morning as a free woman, Casey watched the sun rise over the Gulf of Mexico.

After Casey was released from jail, her first meal was a cheeseburger, French fries, and chocolate milkshake from a Steak 'n Shake drive-through.

CHAPTER NINE

THE AFTERMATH

In the decade since the trial ended, interest in the Casey Anthony murder case has continued. Countless TV specials and true crime podcasts have featured the case. Many people find it just as interesting today as they did in 2008. In a 2018 interview with CNN, Judge Perry shared his theory for why the case is still popular. "[T]here's one question that is on everyone's mind: What really happened? Until that question is answered, there will always be someone searching and someone wondering what that answer is," he said.[1]

There are many theories about what happened to Caylee Anthony. Some people believe she really did drown in George and Cindy's swimming pool. Others think Casey accidentally killed Caylee and panicked. There's even a theory that "Zanny the nanny" was a code phrase for the prescription medication Xanax, and Casey was drugging Caylee with it in order to get a break from motherhood every now and then. But many people

During and after the trial, many people visited Caylee's memorial. Some left behind teddy bears, baby dolls, flowers, and balloons. Many items featured Caylee's favorite characters, including Winnie the Pooh.

still believe that Casey murdered her daughter and got away with it.

Casey's Side of the Story

In 2017, 30-year-old Casey agreed to be interviewed for the first time since the trial. She spoke to the Associated Press about her life since the trial, telling interviewers that she was doing investigative work for Patrick McKenna, a member of her defense team. She also spoke about the public's perception of the case. "Based off what was in the media, I understand . . . why people have the opinions that they do," she said.[2]

Casey also said that even if she had been entirely truthful with the police, she believed she still would have ended up in the same situation. She said this was because so many people wanted to believe she was guilty.

CASEY APPEALS

Casey appealed the jury's verdict convicting her of four separate counts of providing false information to law enforcement. Each count constituted a different lie that Casey had told Detective Melich during two interviews. Casey's lawyers argued that all the lies should be combined into one count since they were related to the same situation. The appeals court disagreed with both the prosecutors and defense attorneys, deciding instead to overturn two of the four misdemeanor convictions.[3] Since Casey had been interviewed twice by detectives, once at the Anthony home and once at Universal Studios, the appeals court ruled that two counts were appropriate.

When interviewers asked Casey about what happened to Caylee, she replied that she didn't know. Casey added that she didn't care what other people thought of her. "I'm OK with myself," she told them. "I sleep pretty good at night."[4]

In 2022, 11 years after the trial, Casey was featured in a three-part docuseries on Peacock called *Casey Anthony: Where the Truth Lies*. The docuseries, which premiered on November 29, marked the first time Casey had given a televised interview to tell her side of the story. Many people criticized Peacock for giving Casey a platform. Nevertheless, people all over the world still tuned in to the docuseries to hear what Casey had to say. In the docuseries, she admitted to being a "convicted liar." "I lied to everyone because that was my whole life up until that point," she explained. "Acting like everything's OK but knowing nothing was OK."[5] Casey also shocked viewers by revealing that the accidental death by drowning story was made up for her trial.

> ### A NEW TATTOO
>
> In the 2022 *Casey Anthony* docuseries, Casey talked about her infamous *Bella Vita* tattoo. "That was my f— you to my family," she explained. Casey said that her father was sexually abusive, and that she was required to pretend everything was fine. More than seven years after getting the tattoo, Casey covered it up with a new tattoo. The new tattoo is made up of flowers and a half-mandala symbol. According to Casey, it symbolizes "growth, rebirth."[6]

In 2017, George told *Crime Watch Daily* that his relationship with Casey was over. "I don't want to see her, I don't want to talk to her . . . I actually lost my daughter and my granddaughter in 2008."[7]

In the documentary, Casey told a slightly different story than the one told during the trial. Casey claimed that she last saw Caylee with George on June 16, 2008, and that he'd handed her the child, who was wet and limp. Casey did not know how Caylee had ended up that way. George was shouting

During a 2017 interview with the Associated Press, Casey was photographed smiling at a picture of baby Caylee hung on her bedroom wall. She also showed reporters framed artwork that Caylee finger painted.

at Casey but then spoke more gently, telling her Caylee would be fine. She believed Caylee was alive because George kept saying that she was. Casey said her father started sexually abusing her at a young age, and that she feared he'd started to do the same thing to Caylee.

She didn't truly believe Caylee was dead until her daughter's bones were discovered in December. Because Casey did not know what happened to Caylee, her defense team came up with the drowning story. But in the documentary, Casey said she doesn't believe Caylee actually drowned. She wondered if her father staged the drowning to cover up his abuse of Caylee. Casey's revelations in the TV series were met with skepticism by most people, especially given her history of lying. Many continue to believe that Casey was responsible for her daughter's disappearance and death.

George denied the sexual abuse allegations brought up during the trial. He also denied the claims that he was aware of Caylee's death and helped cover it up.

In 2023, BuzzFeed News interviewed Alexandra Dean, the director of the *Casey Anthony* docuseries. According to Dean, Casey told her that she was doing accounting and legal assistant work for McKenna. She occasionally communicated with her mother and brother but did not have close relationships with either of them. Dean said that Casey had a

Caylee's Law was first proposed in a 2011 petition, which was created shortly after Casey's not-guilty verdict was announced. Thousands of people signed the petition.

small group of close friends, including members of her defense team, and was living a "small life."[8]

Caylee's Legacy

Casey was convicted of four misdemeanors for lying to the police. But many people thought that Casey deserved a much harsher sentence, even if she hadn't killed her child. As a result of the Anthony case, many states began working on bills to make it a felony offense for a person to fail to report if their child is missing or in danger. The offense would be punishable by a longer prison sentence. The bills were referred to as Caylee's Laws. On January 9, 2012, New Jersey became the first state to officially enact a Caylee's Law. By 2012, more than 30 states were considering adopting similar legislation.[9]

A makeshift memorial still stands at the site where Caylee's remains were found along Suburban Drive. Back when the girl's remains were discovered in 2008, people from all over the country visited the site to pay their respects. Some people built wooden crosses. Others left behind dolls, flowers, stuffed animals, children's books, and notes in honor of Caylee. Years later, people were still visiting the site to remember the happy girl who lost her life too soon.

> ### LIFETIME MOVIE
>
> In 2011, prosecutor Jeff Ashton wrote a book called *Imperfect Justice: Prosecuting Casey Anthony,* which became a *New York Times* bestseller. Later, the book was made into a movie for the Lifetime channel. Starring Rob Lowe as Jeff Ashton, *Prosecuting Casey Anthony* was released in January 2013. Many viewers criticized the movie for reopening old wounds.

TIMELINE

1986
- On March 19, Casey Marie Anthony is born to parents George and Cindy Anthony.

2005
- On August 9, Casey Marie Anthony gives birth to Caylee Marie Anthony.

2008
- On June 16, George says goodbye to Casey and Caylee as they leave the house. He says this is the last time he sees Caylee alive.
- On July 2, Casey gets a tattoo that says "Bella Vita."
- On July 15, George and Cindy pick up Casey's impounded car. It smells terrible.
- On July 15, Cindy places a 911 call to report that Caylee has been kidnapped by her babysitter.
- On July 16, Casey tells multiple lies to the police. She is arrested and charged with child neglect, lying to investigators, and interfering with a criminal investigation.
- On July 17, attorney Jose Baez becomes Casey's lawyer.
- On August 11, meter reader Roy Kronk phones in a tip that he's seen a human skull in the woods near the Anthony home.
- On August 13, police respond to Kronk's tip. They find nothing and leave.
- On October 14, Casey is charged with the murder of Caylee.
- On December 11, Kronk calls authorities again about the human skull he's seen in the woods. This time, investigators locate the skull as well as additional evidence and bones. They believe the bones to be Caylee's skeletal remains.
- On December 19, the bones are confirmed to be Caylee's remains.

2009

- On April 13, the prosecution announces that it will be seeking the death penalty for Casey.

2011

- On May 24, opening arguments begin in the case of *State of Florida v. Casey Marie Anthony*.

- On July 5, Casey is found not guilty on the felony charges of murder in the first degree, aggravated child abuse, and aggravated manslaughter. She is found guilty of four counts of providing false information to law enforcement.

- On July 17, Casey is released from jail.

- On November 15, prosecutor Jeff Ashton's book, *Imperfect Justice: Prosecuting Casey Anthony*, is published.

2012

- On July 3, defense attorney Jose Baez's book, *Presumed Guilty: Casey Anthony: The Inside Story*, is published.

2013

- On January 19, *Prosecuting Casey Anthony* airs on the Lifetime network.

2022

- On November 29, *Casey Anthony: Where the Truth Lies* airs on Peacock. The three-part docuseries gives Casey a chance to tell her side of the story for the first time.

ESSENTIAL FACTS

SIGNIFICANT EVENTS

- On July 15, 2008, two-year-old Caylee Marie Anthony is reported to law enforcement as a missing person. Her mother, Casey Anthony, reports that the child was kidnapped by her nanny, Zenaida Fernandez-Gonzalez, and has been missing for 31 days.

- On July 16, 2008, detectives discover that the nanny never existed and Casey has told them numerous lies. They arrest Casey in connection with her daughter's disappearance.

- On December 19, 2008, bones found in a wooded area by Orange County meter reader Roy Kronk are confirmed to be the skeletal remains of Caylee Marie Anthony.

- On May 24, 2011, the trial of the *State of Florida v. Casey Marie Anthony* begins. Casey is charged with murder in the first degree, aggravated child abuse, aggravated manslaughter, and four counts of providing false information to law enforcement. Prosecutors seek the death penalty.

- On July 5, 2011, Casey is found not guilty on the felony charges of murder in the first degree, aggravated child abuse, and aggravated manslaughter. She is found guilty of misdemeanor counts of providing false information to law enforcement and sentenced to four years in prison. After being given credit for the time she's already served, as well as credit for good behavior, Casey is released from jail less than two weeks later.

KEY PLAYERS

- Casey Anthony was accused of murdering her two-year-old daughter, Caylee Anthony.

- Caylee Anthony was a two-year-old girl who died of undetermined means. Investigators suspected that she was murdered.

- Cindy Anthony was the mother of Casey and grandmother of Caylee. She reported Caylee missing on July 15, 2008.

- Jose Baez was the lead defense attorney for Casey.

IMPACT ON SOCIETY

In July 2008, the news of two-year-old Caylee Anthony's disappearance in Florida pulled at heartstrings across the United States. When the girl's mother, Casey Anthony, was arrested the following day for lying to the police, the story exploded. Reports flooded the media, detailing Casey's bizarre behavior. She hadn't reported Caylee missing for a month, and during that time, she'd partied with friends, gotten a tattoo, and acted as if nothing was wrong. When Caylee was finally reported missing, Casey lied to the police. She claimed Caylee had been kidnapped by her nanny, a person who police quickly realized didn't exist.

Caylee's skeletal remains were discovered in December 2008. Casey was charged with murder in the first degree, among other charges, with prosecutors seeking the death penalty. Millions of people watched the televised trial in 2011. When the jury found Casey not guilty of killing her daughter, the public was outraged. Casey was charged with just four misdemeanor counts of lying to police.

Years later, speculation about the Anthony case continues. Despite a 2022 docuseries featuring Casey's side of the story, many people still believe that Casey was involved in her daughter's death. In response to the Anthony case, more than 30 states have considered adopting a version of Caylee's Law, making it a felony offense for a parent not to report their child missing.

QUOTE

"I remember my homicide team and my crime scene investigations people crawling in the mud, finding little knuckle bones and little finger bones and what have you. That's something that'll stay with you for the rest of your life."

—*Former Orange County sheriff Kevin Beary, who was involved in the Anthony investigation*

GLOSSARY

autopsy
An examination of a dead body to determine the cause of death.

chloroform
A chemical that can cause dizziness, drowsiness, and unconsciousness.

commodity
Something that is rare and valuable.

convict
To find a person guilty of criminal charges.

decomposition
Decay caused by natural factors.

defendant
A person formally charged with a crime.

entomologist
An insect expert.

felony
A serious crime, often involving violence.

forensic
Characterized by the use of scientific techniques to investigate a crime.

homicide
The killing of one person by another.

jurisdiction
A certain area within which a group has authority to make a legal decision or take legal action.

misdemeanor
A minor crime that is less serious than a felony.

obstruct
To prevent, hinder, or interfere with something.

recuse
To excuse oneself from a court case due to a potential conflict of interest.

sequester
To isolate.

skeletonize
To reach the final stage of decomposition in which only the bones remain.

ADDITIONAL RESOURCES

SELECTED BIBLIOGRAPHY

Ashton, Jeff, and Lisa Pulitzer. *Imperfect Justice: Prosecuting Casey Anthony.* William Morrow, 2011.

Baez, Jose, and Peter Golenbock. *Presumed Guilty: Casey Anthony: The Inside Story.* BenBella Books, 2012.

McHugh, Jess. "Meet Werner Spitz, the 95-Year-Old 'Medical Detective.'" *Time*, 13 Apr. 2022, time.com. Accessed 25 May 2023.

FURTHER READINGS

Bithell, Rachel. *The Murder of JonBenét Ramsey.* Abdo, 2024.

Harris, Duchess, and Rebecca Rowell. *The History of Criminal Law.* Abdo, 2020.

Newquist, H. P. *Scene of the Crime: Tracking Down Criminals with Forensic Science.* Viking Books, 2021.

ONLINE RESOURCES

To learn more about the Casey Anthony murder case, please visit **abdobooklinks.com** or scan this QR code. These links are routinely monitored and updated to provide the most current information available.

MORE INFORMATION

For more information on this subject, contact or visit the following organizations:

ALCATRAZ EAST CRIME MUSEUM

2757 Pkwy.
Pigeon Forge, TN 37863
alcatrazeast.com

The Alcatraz East Crime Museum offers information about forensic science and famous cases, such as the Casey Anthony murder case.

AMERICAN ACADEMY OF FORENSIC SCIENCES (AAFS)

410 N. 21st St.
Colorado Springs, CO 80904
aafs.org

The AAFS is a professional society dedicated to promoting forensic science education and improving accuracy and precision in forensic science.

FORENSIC ANTHROPOLOGY CENTER

University of Tennessee
1621 Cumberland Ave.
505 Strong Hall
Knoxville, TN 37996
fac.utk.edu

Commonly referred to as the Body Farm, the Forensic Anthropology Center is a research facility dedicated to the observation and study of human decomposition.

SOURCE NOTES

CHAPTER 1. A MISSING CHILD

1. "Caylee Anthony's Remains Found Steps from Road, Investigator Testifies." *NBC News*, 11 June 2011, nbcnews.com. Accessed 2 Aug. 2023.

2. Ashley Hayes. "Friend: Casey Anthony Was 'Frustrated' with Mother." *CNN*, 1 June 2011, cnn.com. Accessed 30 June 2023.

3. David Ettinger. "Caylee Anthony Remembered by 1,000." *Baptist Press*, 11 Feb. 2009, baptistpress.com. Accessed 30 June 2023.

CHAPTER 2. SUMMER OF FUN

1. Jacqueline Fell, Adam Longo, and Christine Webb. "Prosecutor Calls Ex-Roommates of Anthony's Former Boyfriend." *Ledger*, 25 May 2011, theledger.com. Accessed 30 June 2023.

2. Dennis Murphy. "When Caylee Vanished." *NBC News*, 12 Dec. 2008, nbcnews.com. Accessed 30 June 2023.

3. Ashley Hayes. "Friend: Casey Anthony Was 'Frustrated' with Mother." *CNN*, 1 June 2011, cnn.com. Accessed 30 June 2023.

4. "Testimony: Casey Anthony Partied while Daughter Was Missing." *Florida Times-Union*, 25 May 2011, jacksonville.com. Accessed 3 July 2023.

5. Luke Kenton. "Dark Memories: I Babysat Caylee Anthony." *U.S. Sun*, 22 Jan. 2023, the-sun.com. Accessed 30 June 2023.

6. Murphy, "When Caylee Vanished."

7. "Cindy Anthony Call: 'I Need to Bring Someone In.'" *NBC News*, 10 Dec. 2008, nbcnews.com. Accessed 30 June 2023.

8. Murphy, "When Caylee Vanished."

9. "Extra: Cindy Anthony's 911 Call." *CBS News*, 14 Oct. 2009, cbsnews.com. Accessed 3 July 2023.

10. Barbara Liston. "On 911 Call, Casey Anthony Said Tot Was Missing for 31 Days." *Reuters*, 31 May 2011, reuters.com. Accessed 3 July 2023.

11. Ashley Hayes. "Fireworks, Tears in Casey Anthony Trial." *CNN*, 29 June 2011, cnn.com. Accessed 3 July 2023.

CHAPTER 3. WEB OF LIES

1. Gal Tziperman Lotan. "Caylee Anthony Disappeared 10 Years Ago—and the Casey Anthony Saga Began." *Orlando Sentinel*, 8 Aug. 2020, orlandosentinel.com. Accessed 3 July 2023.

2. Barbara Liston. "Casey Anthony Texts: 'Guess Who Spends Eternity in Jail.'" *Reuters*, 28 May 2011, reuters.com. Accessed 3 July 2023.

3. "4 Times Casey Anthony's Story Didn't Match the Facts." *Investigation Discovery*, 15 Nov. 2022, investigationdiscovery.com. Accessed 3 July 2023.

4. "Casey Anthony Documents Archive – Evidence Released in Caylee Anthony Search and Discovery." *Internet Archive: Wayback Machine*, 14 July 2011, web.archive.org. Accessed 2 Aug. 2023.

5. "Casey Anthony Documents Archive."

6. Dennis Murphy. "When Caylee Vanished." *NBC News*, 12 Dec. 2008, nbcnews.com. Accessed 3 July 2023.

7. "Two-Year-Old Girl Missing for Weeks before Mom Acts." *Columbia Daily Tribune*, 17 July 2008, columbiatribune.com. Accessed 3 July 2023.

8. Steph Watts and Scott Michels. "Mom Charged with Murder in Caylee Anthony Case." *ABC News*, 14 Oct. 2008, abcnews.go.com. Accessed 3 July 2023.

CHAPTER 4. MEDIA FRENZY

1. Jose Baez and Peter Golenbock. *Presumed Guilty: Casey Anthony: The Inside Story*. BenBella Books, 2012. 23.

2. Mike Celizic. "Casey Anthony's Mom: 'I Know Caylee Is Alive.'" *Today*, 15 Oct. 2008, today.com. Accessed 3 July 2023.

3. Ann O'Neill. "Casey Anthony's Trial Is a Summer Obsession." *CNN*, 17 June 2011, cnn.com. Accessed 3 July 2023.

4. Baez and Golenbock, *Presumed Guilty*, 44.

5. Scott Michels, Polson Kanneth, and Lee Ferran. "Caylee Anthony's Mom Released on Bond." *ABC News*, 22 Aug. 2008, abcnews.go.com. Accessed 3 July 2023.

6. "Protesters Jeer at Missing Fla. Girl's Mom." *NBC News*, 22 Sept. 2008, nbcnews.com. Accessed 3 July 2023.

7. Baez and Golenbock, *Presumed Guilty*, 83.

8. "Protesters Jeer at Missing Fla. Girl's Mom."

9. Baez and Golenbock, *Presumed Guilty*, 82.

10. Baez and Golenbock, *Presumed Guilty*, 82.

11. "Anthony Protesters, Fights Costing $4,000-a-Week, Sheriff Says." *NeJame Law*, 30 Sept. 2008, nejamelaw.com. Accessed 3 July 2023.

12. Gal Tziperman Lotan. "Caylee Anthony Disappeared 10 Years Ago—and the Casey Anthony Saga Began." *Orlando Sentinel*, 8 Aug. 2020, orlandosentinel.com. Accessed 3 July 2023.

13. "Uncut: Roy Kronk's 911 Call." *YouTube*, uploaded by WESH 2 News, 9 June 2011, youtube.com.

14. Lotan, "Caylee Anthony Disappeared 10 Years Ago."

CHAPTER 5. THE TRIAL BEGINS

1. "Casey Anthony Wipes Away Tears as Jury Selection Begins." *CNN*, 10 May 2011, cnn.com. Accessed 3 July 2023.

2. Anita Ramasastry. "Why the Judge in the Casey Anthony Trial Was Right to Recuse Himself Due to His Remarks to a Blogger." *FindLaw*, 6 May 2010, findlaw.com. Accessed 3 July 2023.

3. Lizette Alvarez. "Judge Moves Jurors, Not Trial, in Murder Case." *New York Times*, 10 May 2011, nytimes.com. Accessed 3 July 2023.

4. Anthony Colarossi. "Opening Statements Frame Caylee Anthony's Death from Different Perspectives." *Boston Herald*, 25 May 2011, bostonherald.com. Accessed 3 July 2023.

5. Camille Mann. "State Concludes Opening Statements in Casey Anthony Trial." *CBS News*, 24 May 2011, cbsnews.com. Accessed 3 July 2023.

6. David Lohr. "Elisabeth Rogers Jailed for Outburst at Casey Anthony Trial." *HuffPost*, 20 May 2011, huffpost.com. Accessed 3 July 2023.

7. Camille Mann. "Potential Casey Anthony Juror Gets Fined for Speaking to Reporter . . . and Dismissed." *CBS News*, 11 May 2011, cbsnews.com. Accessed 3 July 2023.

8. Colarossi, "Opening Statements."

9. Diane Dimond. "Casey Anthony Bombshell Opening Arguments: Accidents, Incest and Cover-Ups." *Daily Beast*, 13 July 2017, thedailybeast.com. Accessed 3 July 2023.

10. Dimond, "Bombshell Opening Arguments."

11. Jose Baez and Peter Golenbock. *Presumed Guilty: Casey Anthony: The Inside Story*. BenBella Books, 2012. 306.

SOURCE NOTES CONTINUED

CHAPTER 6. WHITE PONTIAC SUNFIRE

1. "Casey Anthony Trial: Dozens Jockey for Coveted Courtroom Seats." *New Haven Register*, 13 June 2011, nhregister.com. Accessed 3 July 2023.

2. Debra Cassens Weiss. "Spectator at Casey Anthony Trial Jailed for Six Days for Giving Prosecutor the Finger." *ABA Journal*, 1 July 2011, abajournal.com. Accessed 3 July 2023.

3. "Dozens Jockey for Courtroom Seats."

4. Ann O'Neill. "Casey Anthony's Trial Is One Hot Ticket." *CNN*, 12 June 2011, cnn.com. Accessed 3 July 2023.

5. "Stench Came from Casey Anthony's Car, Says Her Father and Tow Manager." *CNN*, 27 May 2011, cnn.com. Accessed 3 July 2023.

6. Catherine de Lange. "Casey Anthony Trial: Is the 'Smell of Death' Evidence?" *New Scientist*, 17 May 2011, newscientist.com. Accessed 3 July 2023.

7. "Expert: Tests Show Body Was in Trunk of Casey's Car." *WFTV*, 6 June 2011, wftv.com. Accessed 3 July 2023.

8. "Forensics Expert Gives Compelling Testimony at Casey Anthony Trial." *Inside Edition*, 6 June 2011, insideedition.com. Accessed 3 July 2023.

9. "Forensics Expert Gives Compelling Testimony."

10. "Web Searches Detailed in Casey Anthony Case." *NBC News*, 26 Nov. 2008, nbcnews.com. Accessed 3 July 2023.

11. Yunji De Nies and Jessica Hopper. "Casey Anthony Trial: Did Cindy Anthony Really Search for Chloroform?" *ABC News*, 1 July 2011, abcnews.com. Accessed 3 July 2023.

12. Barbara Liston. "Hair in Casey Anthony's Trunk May Be Caylee's: Expert." *Reuters*, 4 June 2011, reuters.com. Accessed 3 July 2023.

13. Camille Mann. "Casey Anthony Trial Update: Defense Focuses on Scientific Evidence." *CBS News*, 22 June 2011, cbsnews.com. Accessed 3 July 2023.

14. Liston, "Hair May Be Caylee's."

CHAPTER 7. HOMICIDE BY UNDETERMINED MEANS

1. Kyle Hightower. "Lawyers Focus on the Use of Duct Tape." *Herald-Tribune*, 11 June 2011, heraldtribune.com. Accessed 3 July 2023.

2. Hightower, "Lawyers Focus on Duct Tape."

3. Hightower, "Lawyers Focus on Duct Tape."

4. Jess McHugh. "Meet the 95-Year-Old 'Medical Detective' Who Has Examined Famous Cases from JFK to JonBenét Ramsey." *Time*, 13 Apr. 2022, time.com. Accessed 3 July 2023.

5. "Anthony Defense Expert: Duct Tape Not a Murder Weapon." *CNN*, 18 June 2011, cnn.com. Accessed 3 July 2023.

6. "State's Closing: Part 1." *YouTube*, uploaded by WESH 2 News, 3 July 2011, youtube.com.

7. Dennis Murphy. "When Caylee Vanished." *NBC News*, 12 Dec. 2008, nbcnews.com. Accessed 3 July 2023.

8. Yunji De Nies and Jessica Hopper. "Casey Anthony Trial Becomes Heated during Closing Arguments." *Good Morning America*, 3 July 2011, goodmorningamerica.com. Accessed 3 July 2023.

9. Jose Baez and Peter Golenbock. *Presumed Guilty: Casey Anthony: The Inside Story*. BenBella Books, 2012. 404.

CHAPTER 8. THE VERDICTS

1. "Casey Anthony Trial Fast Facts." *CNN*, 22 June 2022, cnn.com. Accessed 3 July 2023.

2. "Casey Anthony Cleared in Daughter's Death." *CNN*, 5 July 2011, cnn.com. Accessed 3 July 2023.

3. Lizette Alvarez and Timothy Williams. "Anthony Is Sentenced to 4-Year Term for Lying." *New York Times*, 7 July 2011, nytimes.com. Accessed 3 July 2023.

4. Breeanna Hare. "'What Really Happened?': The Casey Anthony Case 10 Years Later." *CNN*, 30 June 2018, cnn.com. Accessed 3 July 2023.

5. Jeff Ashton and Lisa Pulitzer. *Imperfect Justice: Prosecuting Casey Anthony*. William Morrow, 2011. 5.

6. Kyle Hightower and Matt Sedensky. "Casey Anthony Release Pushed Back to July 17." *Register Citizen*, 8 July 2011, registercitizen.com. Accessed 3 July 2023.

7. Katie Kindelan and Christina Ng. "Casey Anthony Judge Seals Jurors' Names to Protect Them." *ABC News*, 7 July 2011, abcnews.com. Accessed 3 July 2023.

8. Kindelan and Ng, "Judge Seals Jurors' Names."

9. Doug Gross. "Social Networks Rage over Anthony Verdict." *CNN*, 5 July 2011, cnn.com. Accessed 3 July 2023.

10. Gross, "Social Networks Rage over Anthony Verdict."

11. Mikaela Conley. "Public Irate over Casey Anthony Verdict; Social Media Sites Explode with Opinions." *ABC News*, 5 July 2011, abcnews.com. Accessed 3 July 2023.

12. Kindelan and Ng, "Judge Seals Jurors' Names."

13. Hare, "Casey Anthony Case 10 Years Later."

14. Steve Helling. "Casey Anthony Juror Speaks Out 10 Years Later: 'My Decision Haunts Me.'" *People*, 21 May 2021, people.com. Accessed 3 July 2023.

15. "Casey Anthony Juror No. 3 Speaks Out." *Florida Times-Union*, 7 July 2011, jacksonville.com. Accessed 3 July 2023.

16. Kindelan and Ng, "Judge Seals Jurors' Names."

17. Kindelan and Ng, "Judge Seals Jurors' Names."

18. "Juror No. 3 Speaks Out."

CHAPTER 9. THE AFTERMATH

1. Breeanna Hare. "'What Really Happened?': The Casey Anthony Case 10 Years Later." *CNN*, 30 June 2018, cnn.com. Accessed 3 July 2023.

2. "Casey Anthony Tells AP: 'I Didn't Do What I Was Accused Of.'" *Associated Press*, 7 Mar. 2017, apnews.com. Accessed 3 July 2023.

3. Christina Ng. "Casey Anthony Appeal Reduces Lying Convictions from Four to Two." *ABC News*, 25 Jan. 2013, abcnews.com. Accessed 3 July 2023.

4. "'I Didn't Do What I Was Accused Of.'"

5. Jenna Ryu. "Casey Anthony Is a 'Pathological Liar,' New Series Says. What Does That Really Mean?" *USA Today*, 30 Nov. 2022, usatoday.com. Accessed 3 July 2023.

6. Daisy Phillipson. "Casey Anthony Reveals Meaning behind Cover Up of Tattoo She Got while Her Child Was Missing." *Unilad*, 28 Nov. 2022, unilad.com. Accessed 3 July 2023.

7. Megan Heintz. "Does Casey Anthony Speak to Her Parents?" *In Touch Weekly*, 29 Nov. 2022, intouchweekly.com. Accessed 3 July 2023.

8. Alessa Dominguez. "Casey Anthony's Not Guilty Verdict Shocked America. A New Documentary Says We Got It All Wrong." *Buzzfeed News*, 15 Nov. 2022, buzzfeednews.com. Accessed 3 July 2023.

9. "'Caylee's Law' Introduced to Virginia." *NBC 12*, 26 July 2011, nbc12.com. Accessed 3 July 2023.

INDEX

ABC News, 87, 88
Anthony, Casey
    criminal charges, 6, 35, 36, 38, 43, 46, 77, 82–83, 92, 96
    family relationships, 8–10, 17, 19–25, 55, 61, 93–95
    jail, 36, 39, 43, 46, 82, 88–89
    later life, 92–96
    lies, 18–20, 22–25, 26, 28–33, 35, 53, 55, 76, 82, 87, 92–95
    motherhood, 8–10, 13, 16, 17, 25, 31, 33, 35, 72, 76, 90
    personality, 17, 18, 82
    public perception, 39–42, 48, 85, 86–88, 90, 92–93, 95
    social life, 14–17, 51–52, 76
Anthony, Caylee
    death, 6, 13, 43–45, 51–53, 55, 62, 66, 70, 72–73, 77, 79, 84–88, 90, 92, 93–95
    disappearance, 6, 14, 16, 17–20, 22–25, 26, 28–33, 35, 38–43, 51–52, 55, 72, 82
    early life, 9–13, 17, 76
    legacy, 13, 95–97
    memorial, 13, 97
    personality, 10–11, 18, 51, 97
    remains, 7, 8, 38, 43–45, 51, 62, 67–68, 70, 72–75, 76
Anthony, Cindy, 7, 8–10, 17, 19–25, 28, 31–32, 38, 41–42, 52, 61, 66, 90
Anthony, George, 7, 8–11, 13, 14, 20, 24, 31, 38, 41–42, 52–53, 55, 61–62, 79, 90, 93, 94–95
Ashton, Jeff, 58, 76, 82, 84, 97
Associated Press, 92
autopsies, 74–76
Baez, Jose, 36, 38, 49, 52–53, 55, 77, 79, 80, 84, 87, 89
bail, 35, 39
bail bonds, 39
Bartlett, Matthew, 58
Beary, Kevin, 42, 44–45
"Bella Vita," 17, 79, 93

Birch, Simon, 61–62
bloggers, 40, 48, 56
bones, 6, 8, 44–45, 51, 67, 70, 72, 74, 95
Bottrell, Maureen, 67
bugs, 6, 68–69
burden of proof, 79, 87
Burdick, Linda Drane, 50–52, 79
Campana, Cameron, 17–18
Casey Anthony: Where the Truth Lies, 93–95
Cast Iron Tattoos, 17
Caylee's Laws, 97
child abuse, 6, 35, 46, 53, 55, 82, 93, 95
chloroform, 65–67
CNN, 82, 86, 90
contempt of court, 51, 58
crime scenes, 44–45, 51, 61, 74–75, 77
CSI effect, 77
Dean, Alexandra, 95
death penalty, 46, 48, 84, 88, 89
decomposition, 6, 61–64, 66, 68–69, 75, 76
DNA, 67, 68, 74, 77
drowning, 52–53, 79, 90, 93–95
duct tape, 52, 72, 74–75
evidence, 43, 44–45, 46, 51, 60–69, 72–75, 76–77, 79, 80, 83, 84, 86, 88, 89
Fernandez-Gonzalez, Zenaida "Zanny," 10–11, 18–20, 22–25, 26, 28–33, 35, 90
fines, 51, 58, 82
first-degree murder, 43, 46, 48, 52, 55, 56, 66, 70, 72, 74, 77, 80, 82, 84, 88, 92
Ford, Jennifer, 87–88
Forensic Anthropology Center, 63
Fusion Nightclub, 16, 20
Garavaglia, Jan, 70, 72–73, 75
Good Morning America, 39, 88
Grace, Nancy, 38, 85
Green, Jonathan, 51
Grund, Jesse, 9

Haskell, Neal, 68
homicide, 44–45, 70, 72–73, 86
Hopkins, Jeffrey, 26, 28
Huizenga, Amy, 10, 21
Huntington, Timothy, 68–69

Imperfect Justice: Prosecuting Casey Anthony, 84, 97
impound lot, 20–21, 60–61
interrogation, 32–33, 35, 92

Jennings, Kathi, 59–60
Jordan, John, 35
jurors, 48–52, 61, 76–77, 79, 80, 82–88, 89
jury selection, 46, 48–49, 50, 51

Karioth, Sally, 25
kidnapping, 28–29, 32, 35, 38, 43, 52–53
Knechel, Dave, 48
Kronk, Roy, 4, 6, 8, 43–44, 45, 73–75

Lazzaro, Anthony "Tony," 14, 16–17, 21–22, 29, 32
Lewis, Juliette, 31
Lezniewicz, Nathan, 18
Lieberman, Carole, 85–86
Lowe, Karen Korsberg, 67–68

manslaughter, 46, 48, 55, 77, 82
Mason, Cheney, 72–73, 82
McKenna, Patrick, 92, 95
Melich, Yuri, 32–33, 35, 92
misdemeanors, 82–84, 92, 96
missing person report, 20, 29, 31, 41, 97

National Trial Lawyers Association, 52
news coverage, 6, 36, 38–40, 46, 56, 87–89
911 calls, 20–21, 23–25, 26, 28, 42

Oak Ridge National Laboratory, 63
odor analysis, 63–67
Orange County Jail, 36, 88–89
Orange County Sheriff's Department, 29, 32, 42, 43

Padilla, Leonard, 39, 41
People, 36, 87, 89
Perry, Belvin, Jr., 46, 48–49, 51, 58, 63, 74, 80, 82, 86, 90
Pontiac Sunfire, 11, 20–21, 23–24, 60–69
Presumed Guilty, 49
protesters, 40–42, 84, 88

Rickenbach, Michael, 66–67
Rogers, Elisabeth, 51
root-banding, 67–68

Sawgrass Apartments, 28–30, 32
Schultz, John, 74
Seubert, Heather, 68
sexual abuse, 55, 93, 95
Shaw, Stephen, 68
Sigman, Michael, 66
skulls, 4, 44, 72, 74–76
social media, 40, 56, 76, 84–85
Spitz, Werner, 74–76
State of Florida v. Casey Marie Anthony, 17, 18, 20, 25, 46, 48–53, 55, 56, 58–69, 70, 72–77, 79, 80, 82–84, 86–88, 90, 92–93
Strickland, Stan, 48
Stucker, Ron, 29, 31
Suburban Drive, 4, 6–7, 43–45, 97
Sutton, Natalie, 58
SWAT team, 88–89
swimming pool, 52, 79, 90

tickets, 56, 58–60
Today, 38

Universal Studios, 28, 30–31, 32, 56, 92
Uth, David, 13

Van Susteren, Greta, 63–64
Vass, Arpad, 63–66
verdicts, 77, 80, 82–85, 87–88, 92

Williams, Bobby, 17
Wilson, Polly, 59

ABOUT THE AUTHOR

ASHLEY STORM

Ashley Storm is a writer and a lawyer living in Kentucky with her husband, three mischievous cats, and a flock of bossy backyard chickens who peck on the back door to demand treats. She has written more than 30 books for children and young adults.